PRAISE FOR KELSEY DECKER'S
ADVENTURES OF AWAKENING:

"Kelsey's story is one of those you read and have to take a moment to absorb, to absorb the reality that we, as human beings, can overcome anything if we have the kind of courage and passion that she has. Her zest for life and her authenticity through the darkest of shadows is at once as inspiring as it is fierce and phenomenal. Thank you, Kelsey, for the chutzpah to show us the way through and beyond the adventures of the human experience. Looking forward to continuing the journey with you…"

--- D. D. Scott, International Bestselling Author

ADVENTURES OF AWAKENING:

ALCHEMIZING PAIN INTO PERSONAL EMPOWERMENT

(Adventures of Awakening Book 1)

By

Kelsey Decker

First Electronic Edition: October 2019
First Print Edition: November 2019

eBook and Print Book Design & Formatting by
D. D. Scott's LetLoveGlow Author Services

For little Liliana. To Karen, my guardian angel.

TABLE OF CONTENTS

Preface

"I'm tired of The Kelsey Show," he said. "Everything with you is The Kelsey Show."

His words were repetitive guttural punches, leaving me nauseated and questioning myself.

Was I self-absorbed?

Was everything about *me*?

Was I too much?

Up until then, I'd placed everyone around me on a pedestal. But, for the first time, I was taking center stage in my own life, while together, we floundered through my newfound power.

It wouldn't be until many months later, after our chapter came to a close, that I owned *The Kelsey Show*.

I'd wanted to co-produce, co-star and co-create *with* him. But, he couldn't. He wouldn't. He *chose* not to.

When I started writing this book, and sorting through the last five years of essays, a theme arose. I couldn't believe how many times I'd used the phrase "the show" to describe my life. And these weren't writings he'd read. He never knew that part of me. But somehow, he'd tapped into my psyche and created *The Kelsey Show*, all on his own.

Now…I have created *The Kelsey Show*.

And I welcome you to it.

These are my stories. My journeys. My adventures.

To be honest, I struggled with how much to reveal in this series of books. Somewhere along the way, I got sideswiped with a disturbing feeling. Was I was revealing "too much?" Was it too raw and too real?

In the past, when I'd revealed "too much," it was used against me. People I highly regarded told me I shared "too much, too soon." So, I had to sit with this. Meditate on it. Dance with this too-much-ness. Whether I should hold parts of myself and my story back, out of the fear of making others uncomfortable or seeing myself in a particular light they might not like.

Here's what I came to terms with...

My life has been one hell of a ride. My story is shocking, dirty, fascinating, intriguing, beautiful and uniquely me!

And it's for *all* those reasons that people have said for years that I should write a book.

So, what I decided was that I couldn't hold parts of myself or my story back, or else, I'm not walking my talk. I wouldn't be living authentically me.

Not everyone is meant to share themselves this way, but I believe I am.

All the parts and pieces of *The Kelsey Show* are to be honored, and there's no room in my life for shame around any of it.

The most important part of the journey is my personal road map. It's how I used my own inner compass to arrive at a place of understanding, forgiveness and love for myself. And *that's* what *The Kelsey Show* is all about.

It's about alchemizing pain into personal empowerment. And, I invite you to join me as we embark on this adventure of awakening together!

Introduction

This isn't a typical autobiography or memoir, written in chronological order. These unedited essays, poems and journal entries poured from my heart to paper from 2014-2019. They're a compilation of my thoughts and emotions which I truly believed would never be revealed. Until suddenly, one day, I decided I must compile them into a book to share with the world.

I always knew I'd write a book, but never imagined it would be a series of 7 books, and I certainly never imagined it would be in this format. It's been an intense process, sometimes one in which I felt completely detached from the versions of myself who had gone through all I did. And other times, it's required me to get deep down in the trenches, sloshing my way through the still muddy waters.

I never considered myself a writer and especially not a poet. These titles didn't come easily for me. Proclaiming who you are to the world and more importantly to yourself takes immense courage, which can lead to the ultimate vulnerability hangover. A couple weeks before publication, my body got sick and left me dancing with my demons, yet again, and wanting to run away and live in seclusion on the side of a mountain somewhere, unseen.

It was through my willingness to retreat into myself for that period of time and embrace the ever-present and seductive shadow dance, that I was able to emerge as a beautiful butterfly, ready to be seen and heard, knowing how much my words on these pages would help change someone else's life.

These pages are filled with sex, love, lust, grief, loss, abuse and trauma. But two words I do not believe in are "victim" or "cheating." So, you won't find those in my book. Painful experiences happen. And people have sex with other people. This is an empowered viewpoint. Please tread carefully and without judgement.

Each of the 7 books in this series has 7 chapters, along with a preface for each. You'll also find an accompanying Spotify Playlist at the end of each chapter, as music has always been a way for me to express what my words cannot. So, I encourage you to dive into the music and feel your way through these magical pages.

Kelsey Decker
October 2019

Chapter 1

The Kelsey Show

I shouldn't be happy.
I really shouldn't.
A person like me, with my past, doesn't always go on to lead
a fulfilling, joyful life.

I was born at home in Bloomington, Indiana on July 7, 1981.

Fifteen months later, following my sister's birth, our family of five moved to Elsah, Illinois, where my father taught at the Christian Science University.

We lived in a big white house up a long, winding road. My mother raised rabbits on our wrap around porch, next to fields of wildflowers, without any neighbors in sight.

We had a large deck that sat at the edge of the bluffs, overlooking the Mississippi River. I always had a fear of heights but loved watching the barges move up and down the river, as any five-year-old in 1986 would.

We had sunny days outside, coupled with a house full of secrets inside.

We quickly adapted to my father's short fuse and did our best to stay out of his way.

My memories of that house are vague, other than an extreme bedwetting issue I developed. It grew so extreme my parents tried everything to "cure" me.

One day, my father brought home an electric sleep pad. This pad was placed underneath me in bed and would set off a high-pitched, buzzing alarm with the first sign of wetness. This buzzer woke everyone up, night after night.

All this did was anger my father more, cause an entire household of sleeplessness and annihilate my nervous system.

We didn't stay in Missouri long, and then it was on to Elsah, Illinois. And soon after that, we moved again. This time to Fishers, Indiana. I was starting 1st grade, and our family issues persisted. This move, however, was also an instant change of scenery, going from country house to apartment living. My dad had changed professions and started working in medical sales, quite the opposite of the Christian Science values of avoiding all medical care.

1988 was one for the record books. It was the year I turned 7...on 7/7. Hostility and anger had become pillars in our household. Tears. Fights. Abuse. Those are the things I remember. Not laughter, playfulness or safety.

The year I turned 7 was the year I witnessed my half-brother (we share our mom) being beaten on a repeated basis. It was the year I was shown a "hernia scar" by my father, alone in his bedroom, although he'd never actually had a hernia. It was the year I spent Christmas Eve in the hospital after having my tonsils removed. It was also the year my parents announced their divorce, and the only question I had was "What did I do wrong?"

My mother made the decision to have my brother move to Batesville, Indiana, with his father, out of protection. And my sister and I moved into another apartment with her.

Most of my happy memories as a child were the days in that apartment. My sister and I would dress up and host dance performances in the living room. Our bathroom was covered in flamingo decor, and my mother did the best she could, as a newly single mom of three at age 28.

She would drive on the weekends to pick up my brother, but one weekend things took a turn for the worse. In her physical and mental exhaustion, she fell asleep at the wheel, drove into a ditch, totaled her car and broke her arm.

The next couple years were a blur until the day my sister and I were dropped off at our father's house, to live with him and his new wife. My mother needed some time to get her finances in order, and it was only meant to be temporary.

My stepmother hated us. She never had kids of her own and resented us for moving in on her territory. My father was never without a drink, and my sister and I became anxious and treaded carefully.

I was nine when we moved in with my father, and my bedwetting hadn't ceased. It was during those years, I had to learn how to fend for myself at night. Each night, I'd wake up soaking wet, change the sheets, or more often, find a towel to cover the wetness, change my clothes, huddle up and try to sleep again.

I feared going to sleep, as much as I feared waking up the next morning.

Whenever my father and I were alone in the car, he'd make me hold his hand over the middle console. I never understood this, and it made me queasy. I hated it...and him. Eventually, my hands started over-sweating.

I was taken to the doctor to find out why I was sweating excessively all the time and was told it was my "nerves." So, I was sent to a therapist and prescribed antidepressants...at ten years old.

I never had very many friends because I was painfully shy. I couldn't participate in sleepovers because of my bedwetting, and the only form of escape my sister and I had was to ride our bikes around the neighborhood, filling ourselves with any sense of freedom we could muster up.

We saw our mother every other weekend at whatever house she was living in at the time. We watched her struggle as our father upheld his perfect, upper middle class suburban lifestyle, and each weekend, we begged her not to send us back.

School was also a black pit of despair. Bedwetting turned to sweating. Sweating turned to embarrassment at school, which led to crying. My crying in class became uncontrollable. I was sent to the school nurse's office, where I'd beg to see my mother.

My father had gained custody of my sister and I, at this point, and he'd made it virtually impossible for my mother to see us. She wasn't allowed at my sister's sports games or to pick me up from school.

Back at home with him, my life was getting progressively worse. We were sent to our rooms if our forks made any noise on our dinner plates. The house was to be kept spotless, at all times. We were never to ask for anything.

I spent many days and nights alone in my bedroom, with this feeling of impending doom. I'd leave the lights off and pray nobody would come to "visit."

We weren't allowed to be loud or exuberant. We weren't supposed to be unhappy or cause them discomfort. We had no idea who were supposed to be.

I found solace when I started babysitting for our neighbors across the street from our house. And when I was thirteen, I was allowed to get a job at a pizzeria down the road. This was also the year I finally stopped wetting the bed! My father had found a medication that seemed to cure me. Now that was something to celebrate!

Having a job and being out of the darkness of that house brought me this newfound sense of freedom and exploration, and my innocence drew the attention of a 21-year-old coworker.

His sexual attention enlivened me. It was the most attention I'd received from anyone. A few months of flirtations later, he asked if he could pick me up outside of work and "show me a few things."

I was with my mother for the weekend and snuck out of the house in the middle of the night. I walked down to the corner and hopped into the backseat of his white Ford Bronco. When I snuck out of the house that night, I never intended to have sex. But his hands slowly crept down my pants, and next thing I knew, my pants were off, and even though I was scared, I never resisted.

I walked back down the street, snuck back into the house and made my way to the bathroom. I stood in front of the mirror, holding my stomach and looked down to see blood trickling down my leg. I fell to the floor sobbing.

Shame and guilt settled in, and three weeks later, I called my mother, confessing what I'd done.

My sexual floodgates opened after that. And with this new twinkle in my eye, I attracted the attention of a seventeen-year-old "bad boy" at school. Even though I believed that I was unworthy of being noticed at home, I was perfectly okay with this kind of attention from him.

He gave me rides home after school, which included stops at his house on the way, to explore what it meant to be wild, adventurous teenagers. He introduced me to smoking marijuana, and, oh, how my world began to open up. In the mornings, he started picking me up at the bus stop as well. We'd smoke on the way to school, and I felt so alive and free. But I also got careless and reckless.

It didn't take long for my father to figure out what I was doing. After I didn't come home one day after school, he called around looking for me. I rushed home to find he'd taken everything from my room and stuffed it into garbage bags. He then set the bags on the front lawn and called my mother to pick me up.

My sister had been keeping my secrets, and my only regret that day was leaving her alone in that house.

My mother's inner-city apartment was the complete opposite of my father's suburban life. We lived in Indianapolis across the street from one of the worst schools in the city, didn't have much furniture or a telephone. There were times we went without electricity, too, but I knew she tried. She was the standard, young, single mother, working tirelessly to make ends meet. She'd had three kids by the time she was 23, and now, by her mid 30's, she was exhausted.

I'd spend days and nights alone, in the dark, feeling as though the world continued to cave in around me. To entertain myself, my bad boy would sneak by for visits, until the day my mother caught us alone in the apartment, in a precarious position.

It was horrifying, and she was furious. After that, she made me go to work with her, where I'd sit and wait for her shifts to end. Eventually, I was able to stay home alone again, though I never should have.

I was fourteen, and all I remember about those days was that I wanted them to end, forever. So, one day, I went to the bathroom and grabbed every bottle of pills I could find. I emptied somewhere between 400-700 pills onto the counter, took a glass of water and swallowed them all. I sat down on the couch and went to sleep, hoping I'd never wake up again.

Much to my disappointment, I was horrified to find that I did wake up. I had to be rushed to the hospital, where I stayed for weeks before entering a rehab facility. I admitted to smoking marijuana, so I was cleverly diagnosed as a "drug addict." Ironically, my knowledge about drugs was very limited up until that point. But in rehab, I learned everything there was to know.

My stint in rehab started with in-patient care, where I was on "high alert" for being suicidal. I graduated to out-patient care for several more months, leaving school early every day to take a special bus to the facility.

Trust me, being the suicidal girl doesn't do much for your reputation.

The following year, I switched schools and started making new friends. I spent the next three years going to music festivals, getting high on any drug within reach and having sex with anyone who glanced my direction. I was a vegetarian who wasn't eating well, was slightly overweight, had bad skin and was letting my hair get dreadlocked.

During this time, my mother gained custody of my sister, had her first spiritual awakening, I believe, and started dragging us kids around to various spiritual churches, psychic readings and New Age shops.

The spiritual realm really spoke to me, though, too. I felt a deep connection to the spirit world.

I had tarot cards and crystal jewelry and burned incense. I hung with the hippies and was all about peace and love. I began chasing the high.

The year after my suicide attempt, my sister and I received an invitation from our great uncle in Colorado. He asked my mother if we could go on a two-month road trip with him from Denver to Fairbanks, Alaska.

So, when I was fifteen, the greatest adventure of my life began. We flew to Denver and then drove with him all the way north, back down, and east through Canada and then finally back to Indiana.

This was the magical beginning of my lifetime of travels and wanderlust.

Up until that point, I'd hardly been out of Indiana, and it stirred a wildness within me. That summer I turned sixteen, and I became this worldly, free-spirited girl, seeing parts of the country most only dream of. And I had sex on the side of mountains, tripping on LSD, with boys I'd meet in the small towns we stayed in.

I sometimes wonder if my mother thought (and hoped) that trip would change me. And it did, but not in the ways she probably imagined it would. Returning home to the same life I'd had before I left had me falling quickly back into my reckless ways.

At sixteen, I started sleeping with my mother's coworker, who lived across the street from us. Together, we became cocaine addicts. I had little communication with my father, at this point. But in the conversations we had, he always begged me to go back to him, and when I refused, he convinced me I was crazy and denied any wrongdoing at his house. This left me wanting to numb out even more.

We moved again, which would be my third school within my four years of high school. Things got a little better this time, though. We were in a nicer neighborhood and school system. I snagged a steady job at JoAnn Fabrics, working mostly with elderly women. These women took me under their wings and made me feel safe. Work was the only place I found myself wanting to be.

My senior year, my brother introduced me to a boy who lived an hour away in the country. Our connection quickly grew into an actual relationship. We'd spend wild and crazy weekends together, going to concerts and getting high. I had just turned seventeen, and he was twenty-one, when I found out I was pregnant.

What I didn't know up until this point was that he sat on the Pro-Life Committee when he was in school, and he didn't see us having any other option except to get married and have our baby. My mother didn't give me that option, however, and I went ahead with an abortion. He told me he'd leave me if I went through with it, and that's exactly what he did.

I'll never forget laying in that cold room of the clinic, alone and afraid, while the nurse asked me, "Where's your boyfriend, Hun?"

After the abortion, I sunk into another deep depression, feeling so ashamed, so unloved and so abandoned, again.

I continued to find solace in my work and started a work-study program, so I only had to spend half-days at school. Before I graduated, I was making enough money to move out and into an apartment with my brother, who had moved to the city.

The following year, I attended college, only because that's what you did in those days. I was working full-time, in school full-time and traveling to concerts and festivals as much as I could. My brother and I didn't last long living together, however, and I moved again, in with my best girlfriend.

Life was steadily improving, and one day, when I was eighteen, my mother called, saying she'd just attended a weekend meditation workshop, and that it was so profound she'd pay for me to attend the next one. So, I went.

Profound was an understatement. I was finally able to calm my hectic mind and rest my head and heart. The group was so loving and kind, and I felt like I actually belonged somewhere. During my meditations, I had visions of myself becoming one of the teachers, who called themselves *monks*. I shared these visions with the group, and they confirmed it was my life and spiritual path.

When I left the workshop, I vowed to clean up my act and stop the drug use. To assist me, I joined Narcotics Anonymous. I couldn't completely give up all my rebellious ways, though, so I dated several guys within the group, which was definitely against the rules.

And somehow, despite all my drama, I really started to get my shit together.

I finished my first and only year of college, sold all my belongings, left everything and everyone behind at eighteen years old, and I joined the Ishaya's Ascension meditation community, in the mountains of Waynesville, North Carolina.

In the beginning, I felt a sense of belonging for the first time ever. I was placed in a small group of apprentices, who worked on the grounds of the land, in exchange for our room, board and teacher training. Communal living at its best!

We had meetings every evening, where we dove into the workings of the mind, awareness, the "truth about reality" and how to raise the vibration of the planet through meditation. I became involved with a 49-year-old teacher who introduced me to so many new sexual experiences and ways of thinking and viewing life. He was my magic man.

He took me into Asheville one day to visit a psychic. The psychic told me I was going to meet yet another boy, who would be arriving in my life soon, and he would be "the special one." My curiosity was piqued!

I started having visions of him. I knew what he looked like and every day watched and waited for him to arrive. I could literally feel him. And just like that, one day I was standing in the office looking out of the massive picture window, and there he was, walking up the street towards the building. It wasn't long before we started a relationship and were in love.

A year later, the community in North Carolina closed, and my boyfriend and I moved back to a retreat center that had opened in my hometown of Indianapolis. After a short stay there (where I received my first Reiki attunements), we were told another Ishaya's Ascension group was forming up in British Columbia, Canada. I wasn't particularly drawn to go, as much as my boyfriend was, so we said our goodbyes, and he left for Canada.

I was twenty years old, my heart ached, and I felt completely lost without my partner. Since I didn't have any other life plan, and I definitely didn't want to be back in Indiana, I went against my better judgement and followed him. And thus, began my four years of living in Canada.

When I first arrived, there were only a handful of us living in a large house in a suburb outside Vancouver. Within a year, we all took vows and gave our hearts, bodies, and minds to our teachers (or gurus). They were a married couple, who'd originally lived in the community in North Carolina, and considered themselves to be highly spiritually evolved.

When we took our vows, each of us were given a color to wear – white, red or black. We surrendered our English names, replacing them with Sanskrit ones. For nearly eight years, I wore only white clothing, and my name was Sri Lakshmi, even to my family, upon my insistence.

It wasn't long after arriving in British Columbia and taking my vows that I became slightly disenchanted. My on and off again boyfriend, whom I'd followed there, had sex and fell in love with my female teacher, who was married to his teacher at the time.

Any trust I had left for anyone in the world was shattered. Most of all, I lost *all* trust in myself.

During this scandal, my ex was shunned by the community. He was commanded to go back to "street clothes" and be addressed by his English name again. This is when I first started to see just how harsh it could be to not follow the rules. Despite the scandal, though, our teachers bought a property farther north, where we all worked together to open an actual retreat center, where people would come from all over the world for varying lengths of time. I went through my official Teacher Training, spending months on end in meditation, twelve to eighteen hours a day.

All these hours of meditating had my kundalini rising, and my sexual appetite became something fierce. I still chased my ex-lover for years, hooking back up a few times, while watching him pine over someone he couldn't have. I was "placed" into several other relationships by my teachers, for political reasons, and I became a pawn in their game.

Our so-called "spiritual community" became one of complete mind-fuckery, and I was stripped of any personal power I had left. I learned to disregard my intuition, because others apparently knew a way better than I did. I was striving to achieve a higher level of consciousness that it became crystal clear was unattainable. My frustration grew. But this was all part of their subtle brainwashing. This was their hierarchy of control. Only those they wanted to become highly evolved teachers ever became them.

I spent a few of those years in Canada traveling and living in various provinces, as I was directed to do. I did what I was told, without question. I spent years trying to stop my thoughts, trying to be better, trying so damn hard to be someone other than who I was. I tried to meditate away my pain and trauma. Although I was only in my early twenties, I felt like I'd already lived lifetimes.

Feelings arose of how angry I was with my father, whom I hadn't spoken with for 7 years now. If I brought this up in our evening meetings, I was told I wasn't "ascending" properly, and focusing too much on my thoughts. So, I held all those thoughts and emotions inside, like a ticking bomb.

When I was 25, I was directed to go back to the States to a retreat center in San Diego with a group of other teachers. They secured my position through a relationship with a Mexican man, and we'd go back and forth between Mexico and California, leading weekend workshops and building a community of followers.

I bought a new car and was actually allowed to get a part-time job at the Gap Outlet to help pay the bills, as our classes weren't cutting it. We tithed back to our teachers regularly and tried to stay afloat. This little taste of the "real world," after 7 years of living in seclusion within a tight-knit and controlling community, left me wanting more.

I started toying with the idea of moving back to Indiana and being with my family again. I had dreams of having a baby and starting my own family, and the urge was getting stronger by the day. I battled with this decision. When I asked our teachers if I could leave, I received a firm "no." This is when I knew something was really off, and I was angry and confused.

Within the same few months, a very close friend of mine, one of the more "enlightened" teachers at our center, committed suicide…on my birthday. It tore my world apart and shattered my fantasy. *How could someone enlightened kill themselves?*

That was the final straw. At age 26, I mustered up the courage to leave.

My Mexican boyfriend moved with me back to Indianapolis, and we got married. I naively thought he was my knight in shining armor, there to rescue and save me. I didn't know who the fuck I was or what I wanted. So, I helped him get a green card to live in the States, so he could continue teaching, while I figured things out.

While he was traveling and teaching workshops, I started actually living in the world. I spent days working, and nights out, dancing and drinking. Within six months, I abruptly divorced him and decided I had to move on to a new chapter in my life.

I also decided I never wanted to talk about the Ishayas, ever again. I didn't want to think about it or even admit to anyone where I'd been those eight years, or what I'd been doing. Although I was still attached to my Sanskrit name, and still went by Sri for short. (It was my little way of holding onto any sense of self and security.)

It would take another ten years for me to admit to myself that I had been in a cult.

Within six months after my first divorce, I found myself pregnant, by a man who was much like my father. And even though I had no desire to marry him, I convinced myself it was the best thing to do. I went against my gut feelings, again, knowing it was wrong for me and continued my relentless cycle of abuse.

He was from El Salvador but had been in the States for ten years already, although he didn't have a visa. So, I dove headfirst, for the next six years, into this new immigration project. It was the perfect way to simply forget about the eight years prior in the cult, and also forget the dark childhood I still had yet to truly acknowledge and heal from.

In 2010, we packed all our belongings into a minivan, with our fifteen-month-old baby girl, and drove for ten days from Indiana to El Salvador, where she and I stayed for the next year to apply for his visa, before moving back to Indy.

El Salvador is heavily gang-ridden and is one of the most dangerous countries in the world. Living in a third-world country changed me. It forever shaped how I view the world and gave me a whole new perspective on life.

I developed a deep compassion for the way people live, and what they live for. Life for them is simple, and part of me embraced that lifestyle, while the other part of me was miserable. Our mission was just to survive, in the way everyone else struggled to do there as well.

In the end, we went weeks without being able to leave our house. Gunshots and gang violence were the norm, and when it started happening just outside our doors, I knew I had to leave. So, I summoned up all my strength and courage, again, and returned home to the States, with my daughter.

My husband had to stay in El Salvador, as he hadn't received his visa yet. So, we waited for him, living with my mother and stepfather for the next nine months. During this time, I had a strange feeling about what he was doing down in El Salvador, without me. We'd go days without talking, because "the internet was dodgy." And when we'd speak, I could feel something was off.

But just like I'd done my entire life, I chose to ignore my feelings, thinking I was just being crazy.

Note: It wasn't until several years after our divorce that I learned he'd conceived a child with another woman during that time.

After he returned from El Salvador in 2012, he got his old job back, we moved into an apartment and tried to be "normal" again. That's when I also started going through the immigration process for his other two children from his previous marriage. They'd grown up in El Salvador, with their grandparents, and we'd all gotten acquainted during our time there. So, to keep myself busy, I spent another two years getting them visas to come to the States and live with us.

During this time, tensions were high between my husband and I, and the verbal and emotional abuse escalated. From his alcoholism, he grew ever more bitter and angry. After being in El Salvador, something in him had changed.

I longed for a different life, a different experience, and was growing increasingly dissatisfied in our marriage. I decided I would do whatever I had to do so that I could leave.

I joined a local crossfit gym and started my physical health journey. This was the first time I'd really done *anything* solely for me. I lost 60 pounds and felt a sense of community again, something I'd been yearning for. I became mentally and physically stronger than I'd ever been. I was even convinced to prep for a bodybuilding competition and dove fully into the competitive lifestyle, weighing every gram of food I ate. I'd gained some sense of control over myself, my thoughts and my life, and my husband hated this.

In 2014, not speaking any English and not knowing their father very well, my stepchildren received their visas and came to the States. They walked right into our dysfunctional family dynamic. It all became too much for me, and within six months of their arrival, and two years of me planning my escape, I worked up the courage to leave.

It was really the support of my crossfit community, and the friends I gained during that time, who truly empowered me to leave my marriage. I moved out of our home, with my five-year-old daughter, $50 to my name, no car, nowhere to go and a very angry husband, who was dead set on getting revenge.

The grief hit, and I spent the next three months on the floor of a girlfriend's apartment, sobbing uncontrollably. I could barely move and couldn't see a future for myself, at all.

I had nothing.

I felt like nothing.

I was told I was nothing.

Could I possibly get anymore lost in this lifetime?

But just because I had left my husband, the abuse didn't stop. Abuse had become my security blanket, the filter through which I viewed the world.

I met a younger man through the gym, who I started seeing straight away. I would "sneak around," when my daughter was with her dad or my parents, as if at 33 years old I had something to hide, and I took up heavy drinking for the first time in my life.

My younger man introduced me to the underground world of kink and BDSM, and I found it a whirlwind of dizzying intrigue. Our encounters were filled with lust, desire and raw emotion. And it quickly grew into my obsession. With him, I'd forget my life and current circumstances. Without him, I'd pray for it all to end. Our doomed affair was short lived, but after him, I sought out *more* ways I could manipulate my pain into pleasure.

My daughter and I moved out of my friend's apartment and in with my mother and stepfather, once again. I decided my next step was to start working with my mother at her holistic wellness center. Together, she helped me get my colon hydrotherapy certification, and I left for a training center in Atlanta for twelve days.

It was in Atlanta I went to my first kink club, which set a very high bar. I was introduced to the world of rope bondage and fell in love with the beauty and submission of it.

After returning, I spent another year going to local clubs and private parties that were subpar compared to the experience in a big city. But it was thrilling nonetheless, and I got high on the attention alone. I was never there for sex. I partnered with people for pain alone.

I took on a submissive role and would make arrangements to be beautifully tied up in rope, having sessions where I'd ask to be beaten, with floggers and paddles, until I was black and blue. It was all completely intoxicating and thrilling because, this time, I was the one *asking* for the abuse. I was in control.

I'd wear clothes to cover up the bruises and marks all over my body, not wanting to be found out.

Over time, I switched and took on the role of Dominatrix, and I enjoyed asserting control over others – punishing, humiliating and hurting them, in the same way I'd been hurt throughout my life. This was both powerful and cathartic.

It didn't take long, though, for the games to mess with my head. I would get so high from the pain and then crash into bouts of depression and anxiety. Up and down I went, over and over, as any addict does.

I met another man during this time, who ended up being a culmination of every relationship in my life until that point. We had absolutely nothing in common, except an insanely passionate, sexual connection that intrigued us both. He lived in Cincinnati and came to Indianapolis for our first date. A few weeks later, he flew me out to New York City for the weekend. I felt like a million bucks! So, I overlooked our mountain of differences, as well as the never-ending red flags that went up that weekend, and I let him shower me with affection.

For the next year, we would have wild weekend rendezvous, confusing lust for love. Confusing his adoration for me for his own self-indulgence. He was masterful at his game, getting into my mind and manipulating me in ways that left me feeling as if I were going completely mad.

It was during these years that anxiety started to plague me. Crippling, excruciatingly painful anxiety. In his presence, it was heightened, but it was especially heightened when I was out of his presence. The long-distance only made matters worse.

I took to smoking weed for the first time in eighteen years to calm my nervous system. I was a complete trainwreck.

Despite it all, I kept going back to him, not trusting the sensations in my body, screaming at me that something was off. Because he wined and dined me, I didn't listen. To me, the high was worth the pain, in more ways than one.

We jetsetted to Cancun, Mexico for my 35th birthday, where we spent three days high on MDMA (ecstasy), and to Miami a month after that, for more drugs and sex. That's where the love/lust line grew increasingly blurred.

We took wild weekend road trips together, and when we didn't, I'd pathetically spend my weekends driving to his high-rise condo in Cincinnati. That became my exhausting new normal, not allowing myself the alone time I needed when my daughter was away with her dad.

I was completely lost to myself, again.

I was constantly triggered, feeling worthless, feeling like a terrible mother, and anxious.

Our relationship came to a head one night as the worst panic attack of my life set in. I left his condo at 3 AM, barely able to drive, sobbing and coming to the realization I needed help.

I was awakening to the radical honesty within that I was the one repeatedly putting myself in these situations.

One day, I was walking with my mother through the park and telling her I needed help, describing the exact person I thought would be ideal. Through work, I'd met a woman who I knew was a psychotherapist, and I'd asked her for a referral.

Instead of referring me out, we decided to work together, and she was the exact person I'd been calling into my life. In the beginning, I saw her three times a week. She was my guardian angel, and, together, we saved my life. We began to break it all down. We went back to the beginning. Back to when all this started...when I was a child.

And over the course of the next few months, I would learn more about myself than ever before. With her guidance, we fit all the puzzle pieces together, and I embarked on my healing journey. She helped me see I was never crazy, and not at fault, but I *was* the one in control now. That I had the power to own just how special I am.

Not surprisingly, the toxic relationship came to an end on December 2nd, my daughter's birthday, and it soon became clear to me that I needed to do something for myself. Something I'd never done before and that my heart was yearning for. I knew I had to go on a trip, *by myself*, to a far-off destination. I needed to go on a pilgrimage to "find" myself.

And, for the first time, I honored and trusted my intuition.

In February 2017, I went alone to Iceland for ten days. Planning the trip was as exciting as the trip itself. The adventure of not knowing how I'd come up with the money, take the time off work, leave my daughter and travel further than I'd ever been before, *on my own*, was thrilling!

I experienced the power of manifestation and the law of attraction at their finest.

During my days in Iceland, I hardly spoke to anyone. I spent the days driving around in the land of fire and ice, in the frigid temps, experiencing a level of bliss I once thought insurmountable.

In the middle of nowhere, I learned to trust myself. I discovered just how capable I'd become. I realized that if I'd come this far and survived, there wasn't anything I couldn't do. I learned that the only one standing in my way was me. I was the one who'd broken my heart, over and over throughout my life, by not trusting myself. And I refused to be broken anymore.

I discovered my voice. I started writing. In the silence of that winter wonderland, my inner child and goddess cried out, pleading with me to be heard.

In Iceland, I learned that everything would always be okay. Whatever trials and tribulations this life brought I would no longer suffer the way I had been for so long. I was tired. I was exhausted from fighting – mentally, physically and spiritually. I was done being at war with myself and others.

I returned from Iceland a changed woman, and I knew nothing would ever be the same again.

The weeks after returning were difficult. The high soon wore off, and I sunk back into depression, although a different kind. It was hard to return home to the same outer world, figuring out how to integrate my new state of being within that world.

I prayed and asked the Universe for guidance. I asked for my next step to reveal itself, and every time, I heard the word *Qoya*.

I wasn't sure why I was receiving this message, but the word was familiar from years before, when my mother had told me about a *Qoya* training she'd participated in. I knew *Qoya* was a form of movement and dance, but other than that, I knew nothing. So, I did my research, and it just so happened a teacher was going to be in Indy within the next two weeks teaching a series of classes at a local studio! I couldn't believe the timing.

I attended a couple of classes, and during that time, I also invited my last partner back into my body, and life. At first, I kept my emotional distance, telling myself it was just for sex, but I knew I couldn't keep up that facade for long. I needed to prove something to him. I desperately wanted him to see how well I was doing, so I could validate something within myself. But it didn't take long to see that our encounters and communications started triggering all my anxiety again, and luckily this time, I listened to the truth of my body.

I sat on my knees on my bed one morning before a *Qoya* workshop, with my hands in prayer. With complete reverence, I said out loud:

"Please only allow people and things in my life that are for my highest good."

I had no idea where these words came from, but they were the most powerful words to ever leave my lips.

After the workshop, he and I had plans to meet at my apartment. He'd driven in from Cincinnati, and tensions were high from an earlier conflict. I'd been feeling he wasn't being honest with me on a few things, and shortly after he arrived, our conversation turned into a confrontation.

My intuition had been correct, and I strongly asked him to get the fuck out of my house. This time, I harnessed the power I'd felt in Iceland and used that energy to stand up for myself. I never looked back and have never had a desire to see or hear from him since.

My prayers had been answered that day when I prayed to "only allow people that are for my highest good in my life!"

What had just happened?!

My reality was shifting!

I was still seeing my therapist twice a week, and eventually, we got it down to once a week. After attending several *Qoya* classes and having such a miraculous experience of prayer, I felt the call to become a *Qoya* instructor. I just knew this was my next step.

I started with the online training and witnessed how rapidly my life was starting to shift and change before my eyes. Within a month, I made my way to St. Louis, for the second part of the in-person training. As I was preparing for this Initiation Training, I had no idea how I was going to pay for it, and I was anxious about more traveling, which my job did not afford me.

A friend told me about a website, where you meet up with men and receive money in exchange for spending time with them. I was hesitant, but she was having loads of fun, and making tons of money, so I decided to go for it, with her guidance.

At first, I enjoyed the thrill and game. It was reminiscent of my times in the kink community. The first few hotel rendezvous were exciting. However, my initial intrigue was quickly taken over by a feeling of degradation.

Until I shifted...yet again...

I found myself in two unique dynamics, with two different men, who completely adored me. And it became more than just sex. One of them gifted me the money for my *Qoya* Initiation, knowing that after I returned, our relationship would end.

The other man, I continued to have encounters with. We had a bond, kinship and a mutual respect. And it was a connection I deeply cherished. Ironically, over the next couple years, our relationship turned into one of a beautiful friendship.

By July, I'd manifested the money and time (only four months after Iceland) to take a 10-day trip to Colorado, en route to New Mexico for my birthday, and the third and final part of my *Qoya* Teacher Training.

Part of the draw was to meet the founder of *Qoya* – Rochelle Schieck. I knew there was no way I could teach these classes, and be a part of this community, without making sure I wasn't getting myself into another cult.

To my great joy and delight, I found her and the entire experience to be nourishing. Rochelle never put herself on a pedestal, and didn't expect or want that, and my admiration for her, and her Soul Work, grew increasingly.

Through the teachings and practice of *Qoya*, I remembered how to become present again. I discovered how to feel into my body and how to trust the physical sensations of truth that arise. Through movement and dance, I remembered my true essence as a Wise, Wild and Free goddess. And I became that goddess.

The last day of our week-long training, we did a little exercise with a partner in class, where we put our greatest dreams and intentions out into the world, and our partner mirrored them back to us. For the first time, I felt clarity, and I stated out loud my life-long desire to host women's retreats around the world. Rochelle happened to be my partner, and she mirrored back to me an even greater vision, which included meeting a man, who shared in my dreams.

I left the sacred lands of Taos, New Mexico that day and spent the last night of my journey in Albuquerque, alone. God, how I loved being alone at that point. Through my travels over those months, I'd loved every little thing about solo travel and all the things I was discovering about myself on these trips.

It was also the night before my birthday, and it was time to celebrate! I went out to eat and met two other solo travelers, whom I had beautiful conversation with, and yet, I couldn't shake the feeling that I was meant to be with someone else that night.

A girlfriend had been trying to get me on *Tinder* for a couple years, but I'd been resistant, not loving the online dating scene. But this night, I decided to go for it. Ever since I'd left the retreat earlier that day, I felt on top of the world, in my full goddess power. There was a confidence surging through me like never before, and I knew I had absolutely nothing to lose!

I chatted with several men on the app, and then came across one who stood out, and the timing aligned. The moment he walked in that bar and we locked eyes, it was like the heavens parted. I felt at ease, talking endlessly, and his affection flowed generously. We made our way back to my hotel room, where we spent hours blissfully entangled.

I'd scheduled a hot air balloon ride over Albuquerque for my birthday early the next morning, and he had to be up for work, so we exchanged phone numbers, as little butterflies fluttered around inside my belly. *This one was different.*

After I returned home to Indy, we started frequent communications. We'd chat in the evenings, staying up through the bewitching hour, drinking each other in, over the phone. Within three weeks, he flew to Indy for our first of many magical weekends together.

We rented a cabin in the woods and experienced something otherworldly that first weekend. We were high, without the drugs. We didn't need them when we were together, in the beginning. I was completely enamored. This wasn't purely sex. We actually meshed. He loved listening to my stories, and we talked about traveling, spirituality and all the things that made my entire body light up. We shared a love of being outdoors, hiking and adventuring into the unknown.

A month later, we met in Colorado for another incredibly special weekend, visiting Garden of the Gods and Pike's Peak.

It was after Colorado, though, that he revealed parts of his past that he'd never mentioned before that came with red flags. I wasn't comfortable with how forthcoming I'd been, considering how much he'd seemed to have withheld from me. But I chalked this up to my pattern of revealing too much too soon. And perhaps I did.

So, we carried on, and not long after, he returned to Indianapolis, yet again, and met my daughter.

By October, he'd relocated from Santa Fe, New Mexico to Indianapolis, to live near us. It was a whirlwind romance.

During our time together, we traveled to Europe, hiked the Narrows in Zion National Park, went crystal mining in Arkansas and dreamed about the future. And the longer we were together, the clearer I got on how I wanted my future to look, which didn't seem to align with his. Living in Indiana proved to be difficult for him, with a new job and without the mountains.

(Note: Also, at that time, our family doctor had reported my daughter to child protective services for suspicion of sexual abuse at her father's house, which ended up having no merit, but was highly disturbing. And a few months later, my grandmother passed away unexpectedly.)

Although the magic was palpable and on paper we seemed to fit, something was off, and he wasn't willing to do the deeper inner work I now required for the relationship, based on the diligent inner work I'd dived into. My anxiety had slowly been returning, and I only knew this because I started smoking weed again to ease the uncomfortable silences between us. This was the red flag I was finally able to honor, and a year and a half after we met, we unfortunately parted ways, on December 2nd, my daughter's birthday.

He'd moved in with my daughter and I, and that final night, asking him to leave was one of the hardest things I'd ever done. One of my rules as a mother was to not introduce my daughter to anyone who wasn't going to stay in our lives, *as if we really know that*. It tore her little world apart, which tore me apart even more. As much as my heart ached, though, for all of us, I felt something shift immediately with the ending of the relationship.

I always say your dreams are only as big as the container they're being held in, and the glass around me had shattered, my vision exploding.

The Spiritual Travel Agent blog had been born the month before, with little direction of where it was headed, but I suddenly became aware of what I needed to do. I decided to share more about my journey, my stories and spiritual practices, so I created a Facebook Group to be able to build a community and connection point for those going through the adventures of awakening.

I started taking even more online courses and joined coaching programs to help manifest my vision of guiding other women along their paths.

Then, in January 2019, I had to make a hard decision. My ex and I, while we were together, had planned a trip to Prague in the Czech Republic. I had to decide whether I would still go on that trip, knowing he would most likely be there, too.

Against the judgement of a lot of people I knew, I booked myself a separate Airbnb and went on the journey alone. We awkwardly saw each other on our flights and even met up for dinner, which quickly escalated into a negative experience.

Abruptly leaving the restaurant, we had a love scene made for movies. We stood on a cobblestone street in the most romantic city I'd ever seen, after dark, with hardly another soul around. With tears streaming down our faces, with a cauldron full of love, anger and resentment coming to a boiling point, both with so much to say and yet the words were unable to form.

As I finally spoke, I tried *so* hard to make him understand me. I was desperately trying to prove myself – prove my worth and value – to a man committed to misunderstanding me.

In that moment, I floated above my body and couldn't believe what I was witnessing. I saw myself in this flustered state, feeling completely powerless…and I just watched…

As I hovered outside of my body, I made a vow to myself:

I vow to *never* feel the need to prove my value or worth to anyone, ever again.

I'd spent my whole life trying to please everyone around me. Doing things against my will, against my own inner guidance, against my gut instincts. Against myself. And I was done.

I landed back in my body and walked away, thinking that would be the last time we'd ever see each other, there on the streets of Prague.

Note: I kinda forgot we were on the same flight back home...ugh!

I returned to my apartment in Prague after 30 hours of traveling and no food, emotionally and physically spent. I collapsed into heaving sobs and paced the room. Fatigue, grief and darkness don't begin to describe the loss I felt that evening.

The loss of him and the recognition I'd almost lost myself, yet again.

The next morning, I got up and explored Prague on my own, with fresh eyes and the excitement of a child, even with my emotional hangover.

Synchronistically, I met a beautiful Norwegian woman who I clicked with, on a guided tour. We spent the next couple days eating, laughing, walking and crying together. She had just ended a long-term relationship and had come to Prague to clear her head. We bonded and shared our histories, our heartaches and our strength. We turned what could've been a sad weekend for us both, into a weekend of healing and hope. We alchemized our pain into a beautiful connection.

Right before I'd left for Prague, I'd given my notice at my mother's holistic health center. I loved my job, connecting with people every day, coaching them in life and digestive health. I enjoyed my clients, many of whom became friends, and I'd learned more about the mind-body connection than ever before.

But, I felt this chapter of my life was coming to an end.

I gave my mother my 90-day notice and was soon to embark on the hero's journey of full-time entrepreneurship. Within a few months, I hosted my first women's retreat outside Sedona, Arizona. Planning and executing this retreat on my own was exciting and terrifying, but I embraced every moment of it. Still mourning the loss of a relationship to a man I deeply loved, I dove into my Soul Work, and even deeper into my inner healing.

I invested in more coaching, and over the next six months, built a business helping others alchemize their pain into personal empowerment. I combined all the healing modalities of my past twenty years and created a magical road map to healing.

My life had come full circle.

Someone like me doesn't usually get to be happy.

Physical, sexual, emotional, verbal and financial abuse, spanning thirty years, are what break a person down. Sometimes, they never recover. And yet…here I am. With an inner experience of joy I never thought possible. Living my most authentic life, in complete gratitude. Gratitude for *all* of it.

Someone like me, with my past, shouldn't be happy…but I am.

I'm perfect in every way, flaws and all, traumas and all.

I've learned how to love myself in a deep and profound way. I've learned how to alchemize pain into beauty and hope. I've learned that through it all, I always had (and always have) magic brewing inside me. And that no matter what I've been through, what life has bestowed upon me, I have a right to be happy. And…so do you.

I'm here to show you it's possible.

Soak in and feel the magic of this Spotify Playlist I created for The Kelsey Show:

https://open.spotify.com/user/1265771279/playlist/2Dh7TLJMsn gSzBPr9Vo1wm?si=qmTIkH1LQuOPYUT1UZb-EQht

And here's another bit of magic with my Spotify Playlist for Prague:

https://open.spotify.com/user/1265771279/playlist/6jj0EM9Zsbu RNSYu3U7arp?si=eWBwFlOwT6-zz1cMelnK2g

Chapter 2

The Lost Boys

The Lost Boys.
Connections that were palpable.
Electric energies.
Magnetic frequencies.

The Lost Boys were pieces of me. And as much as I blamed and shamed them for the emotional, physical and verbal pain they caused, they were simply my muses. I spun circles around them as I twirled around this world.

They were my salvation.
I lived for them.
I longed for them.
And I lost myself to them.

I was an addict.
Addicted to making them special.
Desperate for their affections.

They were all searching and wandering, with no true north. And in me, they found a home, if only temporarily.

My own moral compass both excited and terrified me. My dreams and visions of The Lost Boys blurred my reality, causing me to indulge in a world of fantasy and intrigue.

I poured my soul into fixing and healing them, and it might've been incomplete, but in my own special ways, I accomplished that.

Each one tore me apart. And with each ending, I was left gathering up the fractured pieces of my heart on the floor.

In 2014, I started writing about them, and through poetry and prose, I processed my pain.

That's when they became...The Lost Boys.

What If

What if you text me
And ask me how I am
And I'm not okay

What if I don't pretend
Will you still find me alluring

What if I'm not giggly and I'm not bubbly
Will you still want me

What if I'm crying, eyes red and skin blotchy
Will you still find me sexy

What if I told you it took everything for me to get out of bed this
morning
Will you still respect me

What if I said I missed you
Will you continue to be distant

Today I Hate You

I heard about you. And I know you've been hearing about me.

You contacted my best friend while I was out of town. You'd probably heard I was in Atlanta doing well and decided to fuck with my head.

You two had never even spoken before, and suddenly, you needed to help her with a problem she posted about on Facebook. Luckily, she knows me well and waited until I returned to tell me.

I cried right there in the middle of the restaurant. And for some reason, amidst my anger, I felt sorry for you.

Several weeks passed, and I'd let it go as much as I could, but then you did it again…

This time, you inquired about seeing naked pictures of her. She never responded and sent me the screenshot of the conversation.

Again, I cried on the spot.

Why were you doing this? Were four months of mind-fuckery not enough for you?

It's been nearly another four months since I left your house that day. Not one text, phone call, message or interaction since.

I'm sure you weren't expecting that. I'm sure you were expecting the weak little girl I was around you, to cave in and beg to see you, fuck you or ask you to beat me. But I didn't. I've stayed strong.

I knew I was going to run into you. I could just feel it. Everywhere I went, I felt on edge. This city isn't all that big.

And then it happened.

You knew I'd be working the body building competition that Saturday. I always worked those shows for my coach. There I was having a great time schmoozing and being my upbeat self and then...I saw you.

You walked through the door, and you didn't see me at first. I felt paralyzed and tried not to watch you from the corner of my eye. You saw me from across the room, and your look of shock wasn't subtle.

And then you did it...

You immediately turned away, held onto your girlfriend and walked in the other direction. No acknowledgement. No hello or casual small talk. No smiles, even in your eyes.

There was nothing.

It took every ounce of strength in me to keep my shit together and continue the long, 14-hour day without acknowledging the panic attack I was silently having.

You're a coward.
You're a pussy.
And you are an asshole.

Have you heard about how well I'm doing now? My guess is you have.

Do you know the ending of our fucked-up dynamic was the best thing that ever happened to me?

And that, most of the time, I'm happy you decided to fuck around and explore "being poly" because it gave me a reason to leave.

Do you know that after I left, I fought harder than I've ever fought before to pull my shit together and get my life straight…and I did it?

That I'm now successful and happy and confident?

I wish I could thank you for being there for me after my divorce and for being my friend. But I can't.

Not today.

I wish I could say I'm grateful to you for introducing me to the kink community and awakening this beautiful sleeping beast within me.

But not today. I just can't.

I wish I could be happy that meeting you gave me the courage to finally leave my miserable marriage. I didn't do it for you, but you knew you were the catalyst.

But I'm not happy about that today. I'm just not.

And I wish I could see the perfection in all that transpired between us. But you know what?

I can't. Not today.

Today isn't one of those days. I don't even want to.

Today…I just hate you.

The Show

They all want to touch
But they don't want to pay
The price
Of admission

I put on my face
The one that they like
Smile for the camera

The line gets longer
For the circus is in town
They want to watch the show

I spin
I dance
I fly
I drop

And they witness
In amusement

There's no net when I fall

Move On

If you think I'm fascinating
Move on

If you think I'm intriguing
Move on

If you think I'm cute
Or beautiful
Or amazing
Move on

If you know I'm too much woman for you
Move on

Or if I'm too well traveled
Too smart
Too ambitious

If my heart is too big for you
Move on

If you think I'm too good to be true
I am
So move on

Because my heart is too big
My mind is too open
I stumble when I fall
I trust without realizing it
And then it's too late

Because I'll turn cold as ice
You won't know what hit you

When you realize I'm just too much

Too much woman
Too much heart
Too much love
Too much laughter
Too much pain
Too much strength
Too much fun

And way too many wild ideas

My heart is restless
My body on fire
I will burn for you
But I will also burn you

So if you can't handle the heat
Move on

If you know I shine too bright
Move on

If you know you'll never be enough for me
Then move on

Don't play games with me
Don't make me question
Or wonder where we stand

I'm too old
I'm too tired
My heart too fragile
And my mind too complicated

If you want to be real with me

Then stick around

But if not
Please, just move on

I'm sorry

I'm sorry
I wanted more than you were willing to give

I'm sorry
My heart contains more love than I know what to do with

I'm sorry
I changed the game and you changed the game
And in the end nobody got to win

I'm sorry
I don't know how to open up and detach at the same time

I'm sorry
We got along so fucking well

I'm sorry
I couldn't maintain a friendship without compromising myself

I'm sorry
You started to care and then I started to care

I'm sorry
That because of it I can no longer be there

I'm sorry
I will always question if I made the right decision

I'm sorry
For all the conversations that will never be had

I'm sorry
My emotions always get the best of me

I'm sorry
All I want to do is pick up the phone

I'm sorry
My heart hurts and I'm feeling all alone

I'm sorry, I'm sorry, I'm sorry

Those words will never quite be adequate
For what I want to say

I'm sorry
I'm angry and sad and confused

I'm sorry
You couldn't get clear on what you wanted and I had to choose

I'm sorry
You know me so well, but will never fully understand where I
was coming from

I'm sorry
You met every requirement on my checklist
And it's a big list and that's a rare thing

I'm sorry
I will always wonder where you are and what you're doing
I will always wonder if I could have made it work

I'm sorry
You made me a better person
You brought out the best in me, always

I'm sorry
I wasn't needy or jealous
I didn't beg for affection

But you gave it willingly

I'm sorry
I liked when you held my hand

I loved to kiss you
I loved sharing my stories with you

I'm sorry
We were so comfortable with each other
And it's hard to imagine that with someone else

I'm sorry
I will never know what was going through your head
Or understand why you did the things you did

I'm sorry
I needed consistency

I wasn't asking for much
I never did
I was different with you

I'm sorry
I'm grieving the loss of us

The loss of someone I knew such a short period of time
And yet someone very special

And I'm sorry
There will always be a place in my heart
That's carved out just for you

The 7-Year Itch

They all told me that if I could wait just one more year, the 7-year itch would be over. Like somehow everything would magically change.

But I was done.

I had been done for a very long time in my heart and my head. I knew no amount of time or therapy would change that.

So, I eventually left.

I'd been threatening to leave for months, and, at one point, I did, only to go back. He'd threatened to leave for months before me, but only when I finally made the choice, did he beg me to stay.

These past ten months have brought about more uncertainty in myself and in the world than I've ever experienced.

Each day is a struggle, and I long for the peace I once profoundly knew. But, I know someday I'll look back at this time and be proud I made it through.

Today, would've been our 7-year wedding anniversary. 7 is a special number to me, so it feels significant.

There's no expiration date on grieving, but, lately, there just seems to be so much to grieve about. Too many endings and not nearly enough beginnings.

But...amidst the tears, I'm going to choose to be grateful.

I'm grateful we're friends now, and I can't imagine my life without him in it. I've never wanted him back or wanted us back.

But, at one point, he was my best friend, and it helps to know he'll always be there.

There's only one place to go in the next 7 years…and that's up!

Time Will Tell

What happens when you take
Sex out of the equation
What is to come when faced with
This type of situation?

When it started as sex
But don't leave out the great conversation
Late nights talking, drinks
High intensity flirtation
Hands holding, bodies mingled
Even in the bar

And on the walk home
You never wandered far
Things progress

Even with minimal time together
You realize this isn't just sex
It's more than the panty-dropping texts
Emotions get involved
And you're not sure what comes next

You hope for more
But maybe only out of habit
Sometimes it's hard to distinguish

All your ideas of how things look are blown
And as your past dictates
When you push for more
You end up alone

So you look within
You start a new journey

You realize some connections
Are worth unlearning

Everything you ever thought you knew
Of how it should look
And you decide to write a new chapter
In your book

But you wonder what will happen
Can you really make it work
Can you make peace with this decision

Will your natural instincts kick in
Or have you really flipped the switch
Some people make you more whole
They inspire you to sew yourself
Back together stitch-by-stitch

Knowing this change is for the best
Because in giving up this one thing
You'll get everything you ever wanted
In what's left

It's hard to know how this tale will end
Because sometimes our true loves
Are really just our best friends

In The Dark

In the darkness
Their faces haunt me
Their voices taunt

In the stillness, though, I hear only Him breathe
His heart beating

In the quiet
I can smell Him
Taste Him
The longing makes my body ache

In the darkness
I love to hate them
Their words cut
I want to bite those soft lips

I want to scratch and claw

In the stillness
I can't breathe
I suffocate in the lies
And yet I long to look only in His eyes

In the quiet
I am screaming
My thoughts of them just too much
Each one so special
Each one so charming
But it's He that consumes me
Won't escape my mind

Leaves me wanting more

Always more

But in this room
In the light of the day
There is only me

I must learn to close those doors
Keep them shut
And throw away the keys

Let Her Be

She shuts the world out
It's better that way
Her wounds have gushed open
And it's best if you don't stay

She will never trust you
She will never believe
It's best not to take her personally

When she shuts out the world
It's for everyone's good
She needs to go inside
To where she can be understood

Memories flood her precious mind
Your words can't make it better
Your love for her feels cheap

Good intentions fall short
On her cute little ears
She will never allow you
To wipe away her tears

Just leave her be
If you're not up for the confusion
The frustration
The emotions that run deep within her

Her heart has been played
More than she's willing to admit
So she's hesitant about everything
And everyone

She will always doubt
All the things you say
And each little thing you do
It would be impossible
For her to ever really love you

She will never accept what you offer
With an open hand, heart or mind
With every kind word
She will question the motive

With every generous act
She will feel unworthy
So as the past is uncovered
New truths discovered
She needs time to process

If you care
As so many claim
Or perhaps pretend to do

Please know this girl
Will be a whirlwind
Spinning in circles around you

Undeniable

He looks my way and
The world around us
Begins to disappear

Time stands still
Bodies blurred
Sounds muffled
Tunnel vision

The energy is electric
Sparks light the space
Between us
We haven't touched

A certain distance is required
To keep magnets apart
My body burns with desire

Our connection gets me high
The flames that ignite in
The meeting of our minds

I avoid eye contact
But I can't resist
One more look
I'm floating in the abyss

In a place only we understand
Where I go in my dreams
Where our spirits connect
It's undeniable

I hold the space for us

We swim in the infinite
It's effortless
All becomes clear
And we are free

The Vision

I remember him clear as day
Walking up that path
Sandy blonde hair in the breeze
He didn't know, but I was waiting

When we met the heavens aligned
I'd had visions of him for weeks
The Universe transpired to bring us together

He would become my lover
My best friend, my partner

For years we danced together
In the passion that couldn't keep us apart

I taught him things
He was a broken boy

We would walk through the mountains
Sit by the stream on that bridge
Looking out onto the beauty
Of the endless horizon

We were both so young
So far from home
Full of wonder and awe

We fit together
In the crook of his arm
The softness of his neck
I was consumed by my love for him

But what's love without tragedy

Years went by and we went our separate ways
Although never far apart

We both moved on
Went through our strings of habitual pairings
He was never far from my mind

No one else ever lived up to the connection we shared
He has a child now
We talk once or twice a year

Even in those times
We don't get too close
Because with some people you've experienced too much

Too much love
Unspeakable sadness
Events that are best forgotten

We spent years in a place, not many could comprehend
We were different and chose a path unordinary

Our need to experience the purity of life
Always far exceeded our need for each other

I still think of him every now and then
I found an old photograph the other day

In the end he hurt me in a way I will never forget
He shaped my future for a life of mistrust

But my memories of him are fond
All the pieces of him, of us tied together in an infinite bond

My Muses

Muse after muse
What's a girl supposed to do?

After a while they all feel the same
Every word they speak
You swear you've heard before

Do they read this shit in books?

It's all so familiar
Each one you thought was different

Are any of them different?

They evoke such emotion in me
They put me over the edge
They always leave me here
Dangling on the ledge

Each time I open up
I lose a little sacred part of me
Every time I regret
Letting them see

They encourage me so well
Make me feel like such a good girl
For opening up
And sharing my secrets
For wearing my heart on my sleeve

As long as I'm the fun girl
As long as I'm the pretty girl
But nobody wants what's really underneath

There's only so much they can handle

I can't really blame them
I'm not an easy girl to love

Good intentions fall short
Decent people turned fake
Will I ever learn
To stop making this mistake?

So up the walls go
This time I'll build them higher
Maybe more layers
Thicker and stronger

I've gone into my cave
Back to the safety of solitude
It's the only place
Where I really can't lose

The Little Things

I woke up in the middle of the night and missed you.
I rolled over and am not sure why I thought you'd be there.
I guess I thought it had all been a bad dream.
The emptiness of my bed felt enormous.
I just wanted an arm around me.
I just needed your cuddles.

It's nice on my own.
Things are better on my own.
But sometimes, like in the dead of the night, I miss the little
things.

Love, Reduced

Our love has been reduced to a business transaction
I won't fall prey to your kindness
It's back pay for the years I spent in service to you

Memories of you in the doorway
Watching myself cowering in the corner

Never again will that girl emerge

All you have become is a reminder of who I used to be
Your anger swirled around causing chaos
As the baby looked on

Now you think you have her in your grips
I'm no fool to your games
To your sick, twisted web of manipulation

I married my father after all

Your power over me will fade as did my love for him
But you will never take her

I won't allow you to sink your claws into the heart of an
innocent
She will always feel my love
And I will always put on a smile
In between the tears I shed in front of her from you

No longer will you fill me with doubt
Never again will I succumb to your belittling
I will show her what's it's like to be strong
Business and emotions don't mix
And that's all we've become

All I want to feel towards you is numb

He's Gone

He slowly drifted away
Until I felt him disappear

The connection faded
Our minds severed

I can't sense him anymore
A chemistry once so strong
Now he's gone

It was inevitable
It feels like a dream

Just a blip in time
Our memories hurt my heart
He was never to be mine

He's moved on
Of course he would
I don't know how I wanted it to look

Not like this
I'm desperate to let it go
But I'm holding on for dear life

To something
To everything
And absolutely nothing

Alone in this room
I want to curl up in a ball
Pull the covers up
And just feel small

It all seems so silly
I built him up in my mind
Made him, made us
Untouchable

But I guess in reality
It's not really complicated at all

Letting You Go

I let you go
Just like that

I thought it would be harder
But I've gotten smarter

I may hold on
Scratch and claw
Till I finally let go

But once I'm done
I'm done
I'm no longer interested in your show

I've closed some chapters
In my storybook
So that I can move on
And get a better look

I will glance back with a smile
For all that I learned
I gave you everything
Even though it wasn't earned

Thank you for late nights
For holding hands
For endless laughter
And being so drunk I couldn't stand

Thank you for friendship
And honesty
For being my special one
Even if only for a short time

It was fun

Pretending you were mine
Now I've let you go
I only wish you well
Though it makes me sad
To think of the stories
We will never tell

• • •

I let you go today
As I ripped the pages
Out of my book
I turned around
And took a second look

Making sure I was doing the right thing
Doubt as usual
It's what the night seems to bring

When I let you go
I felt kind of free
It was in that clarity
I really began to see
And my heart didn't close

It began to open

In or Out

I could pull back
Let my fear take the wheel
Always wonder what might have happened
What we could have been

I could lose my mind living in the future
Worried about how easily he could break me
Continue with my anxiety
Living my life in apprehension
Keeping my walls up and my heart guarded

Or...

I could let go and be present
Appreciate the happy times
Let my feelings of anxiety turn into butterflies

Lay out the broken pieces of my heart for him to see
Allow us to just "be"
It's a moment to moment choice

And it's a battle of heart and mind
But if I don't open my eyes to what's there
I will forever live blind

Cold Eyes

It's happened four times I can recall over the past year.

Everything with each one was going along well. They showered me with affection, begged me and I obliged. Times were wonderful. Weeks and months went by and we grew closer.

Then, out of nowhere, one day the switch has taken place.

The energy is distant, and his eyes have grown cold. I'd wonder where they'd gone with that far off look. Within a day, I'd wonder who this person was, where never before had I questioned.

They flipped the switch and would never come back. They were gone to me and to the world. And suddenly, where there once stood nothing but confidence, stood a needy little girl.

The 180s had me questioning and doubting everything. I found myself rummaging through old messages to justify how I got to this place. But I came up short.

All I found were the messages from them of friendship, lust, longing for me. It didn't make sense.

Why did they change their minds?
Why did it feel so easy for men to just cut you off?
And out of nowhere?

Do we not read the signs?
Were there signs?
Was it all in our heads?
Did they ever really care?
Why the blackness and the blank stares?

These are the thoughts running through my mind as I lay here with visions of all their cold eyes.

The Stirring

I've seen us dancing under the stars and swimming in the seas
The way you look at me when you think I don't notice
As if we've known each other for an eternity
Not just this lifetime, but many before

You stare in my eyes as if you're touching my soul
Although we've never touched
I can still feel you lingering within every cell of my being

I want to know the parts of you I haven't seen yet
I will listen to your heartache and share my life experience
We will talk of travels, our dreams, the passions that burn within
us
And we will understand each other as we already do

Ours will not be a typical love story
It will be built on a solid foundation of purity
Of souls reunited and recognizing each other

Ours will be a short love affair
You will follow your bliss and I will encourage it
You've come into my life not as a tornado
But smooth and unassuming

We will laugh and share
Fingers intertwined
Hearts fluttering
A poignant piece of history

Bad Boys & Mean Girls

We stood in the living room, both of us overwhelmed by emotion. He held me in his arms, not wanting to go. He leaned down and asked me a question.

"You don't want to be with an asshole, do you?"

I wasn't surprised.

"No, I've had enough assholes in my life. I'm ready for the good guy," I replied.

"That's good," he said. "I'm not an asshole, and it seems as though that's what a lot of girls want. I've only ever been with mean girls. Don't get me wrong, they weren't bad people, but they weren't the nicest, either. But you're different. You're actually nice, really nice."

We'd had the discussion once before about his slew of mean girls. He was engaged to one for five years. He was becoming very aware of being drawn to women that were like his mother, and he was ready to break the cycle. I could relate.

I've had my own share of shitty, abusive relationships that mirror the relationship I had with my father. Yes, I have Daddy Issues.

Husband #2 was pretty much a reincarnation of my father. No matter how much I hated him, he seemed to always pop up in my relationships throughout the years.

From as early as I can remember, I always wanted the bad boys. I think it's a common theme. I had sex and started using drugs at fourteen with a number of bad boys throughout high school.

I've had relationships with a few nice guys since then, but they never lasted. I'm not into pushovers.

But here I was listening to the other side of the story. I don't often hear about guys liking the mean girls. I held him and petted him.

He told his brother how I gave him a massage as if it was the greatest thing on earth. I didn't understand how he'd never had anyone show him genuine affection before. And here I was not able to keep my hands off him.

Hearing this news had only made me want to do more for him. My service sub and my mommy personalities came out in full force. I went back and forth between them. I wanted him to feel what it's like to really be loved, cherished and desired.

It makes me sad to think we go after mean girls or bad boys because of their super-strong allure. Something draws us to them. But ultimately, they don't make us happy and don't fulfill our needs for more than one or two nights.

I could see how he'd played out this pattern because, subconsciously, he didn't think he deserved more. I saw how I'd been drawn to emotionally unavailable men because I didn't think I could get more.

That's what it all came down to…our sense of self-worth.

But now, we've both seen the difference, and we like it. I couldn't ever go back now that I've tasted the forbidden fruit...the nice guy with an edge, the perfect combination.

He will fuck me senseless and take control and then do my dishes and take out the trash.

Now…if only he lived in this city...

The Space Between

It's where I find myself waiting for you
Between a love story and a forever song
Where the days feel much too long

Life carries on without your sweet melody
In the place between my hopes and your memory

This is where I'm waiting
Where I always will
Like a knife
You came in for the kill

The space between weighs heavy on my heart
Not knowing how much more time will keep us apart

My Addiction

He's my secret
I've been keeping under lock and key
I don't want to share him
For I'm afraid I'll wake up from this dream

He was my muse
Now I have no words
Except for the ones we share
In the late hours of the night

In the wee hours of the morning
I have to pull myself from his grasp
Don't tell me what my heart refuses to hear
It's my choice
My head is quite clear

Pain? Yes. It's inevitable
But right now I love us
Trying not to get sucked into our web of lust

He will go away once again
The old familiar dust will settle
But this time I'm prepared
Though I'll admit I'm oh so scared

He's my drug
My addiction
How did I end up with this affliction?

I hate him
I love him
And I hate that I want him

But he brings a chaotic peace to my life
It's not something that can be described

My lost boy

I hope he finds his way
Because no matter what rational minds will say
I can't help but still be there at the end of the day

I'm a fool for love

Your Expiration Date

It's been three months
Since you left me here

Three months
Of frustration, heartache and tears

Three months
That not an hour goes by
Without thinking of you
And those mesmerizing eyes

Three months
Of feeling like a stupid girl
While you are off
Traveling the world

Empty promises
You never keep
Haunt me even while I sleep

I can easily let go
Of all the rest
But you, my dear
You are the test

Three months
Of telling myself I am done
If this were a game
You surely won

Three months
Of your ups and your downs
Being there for you

When no one else was around

Three months of hating, craving and wanting you
Three months too much
What's a girl to do?

Three days more
That's what I'll give
For you to decide
The life you want to live

Be careful with your words
And your actions too
When they don't match up
I'll be done with you

Three days
Before I close the door
On you
On our love story
We've been here before

Three days
And I won't look back
Once I'm done, I'm done
And I'll finally admit to myself
You were never the one

Empty Promises

Before he left, he sucked me back in.
He said he would be here.
I didn't believe him.

I told him we'd been down this road before.
He promised.
I still didn't believe him.

Then we talked about it more and he was relentless in his word.
We made plans.
We set dates.
I made dinner reservations.
I really wanted to believe him.

We talked for two hours every night for ten days.
The day he left he was desperate to get a hold of me as he
boarded the plane just to hear my voice.

Even after he left for his trip, he stayed in touch.
I hadn't expected that.
I was hopeful.

My head knew better.
My heart yearned.
Then the emails got less frequent and eventually ceased.
It was happening again.

I wasn't surprised.
Disappointed? Yes.

I grew frustrated.
I drank and fucked to try and forget.
To tell myself I'd moved on.

I had something to prove.

I refuse to wait around for any man I'd told myself.
But I was waiting.
Again.

I got beat and strung up like a rag doll each time I heard his
voice.
Each day I convinced myself I was letting him go.
Every other minute I'd check my email.
Then the day came I knew he was flying back.
Not one word.

I received an email days later.
It was short saying the airline lost his stuff, including his cell
phone.
He asked for my phone number.
I sent it.
I didn't believe him.
That was the last I heard.

He was supposed to be here a week ago for Spring Break.
I had made arrangements.
My daughter was with her dad.
It was supposed to be perfect.

He never called.
I didn't receive a text or email.
He just didn't show up.

I'm ready for Spring Break to be over.
I'm tired of the reminder.
I'm done with fucking others to convince myself I'm not hurt.
I'm over these three months spent waiting on a ghost.

I knew.

I knew not to believe him.
But he promised.
This time he promised.

Who does that?
Who the fuck does that?

The tension was building, and I finally confided in my mother.
She didn't hold back and said he's just as bad as my ex and that I
had to be done with him.

I broke down.
I finally allowed myself to feel everything I needed to.

And now I'm here ready for a new week.
For a new chapter.
I'm almost relieved.

I will take all the good memories and hold them tight.
Nobody can take those from me.

But he didn't end up being a good person.
Three months ago, I believed in something I never thought I
would again.
Now I don't know what I believe.
I feel lost and yet free.

Change

I've had a habit of thinking men would change for me.
And I've had men who've stupidly thought I would change for them.
But we can't change who we are.
We can't change our experiences that have shaped us.

I desire to be around the ones who will challenge me and inspire me to grow.
I seek out the special ones, the ones who look beyond the surface.

I've always craved those deep connections.
I want to sit and talk and tell stories with you.
I want to hear yours.
I want to know your passions, what drives you.
All the rest is filler.

I have my reasons why I do the things I do.
They may not seem valid to you, but they are mine and mine alone.
My actions are driven from a place of deep ambition, a place of understanding and a place of wanting to do more than just survive in this world.

I may fumble down into a hot mess of a girl at times.
My experiences in life tend to overwhelm me.
But don't underestimate the power in my perseverance.

I won't change for you, but I will grow with you. If that's not enough, then I'm not the girl for you.

What I forgot to tell you

I forgot to tell you that none of this was an accident. I forgot to tell you that I created you, that I manifested you sweeping into my life that evening. I'd put it out to the Universe that very day, driving in that convertible through the desert.

You wouldn't have believed me. My magic both invigorated you and scared the fuck out of you, and you were in a constant battle within yourself, deciding which version of you would win.

In the end, you let the insecurity win. You questioned everything I did, and my motives. But you loved to see me happy more than anything, and your face would light up when I was fully in my goddess power.

But then you'd question yourself, and worse me, and I never understood why you had to do that. Why you had to dim my light to make yourself feel better. And I don't think you ever actually felt better.

You didn't play fair.

When you moved from across the country to be near me, I felt your level of commitment. I never pressured you, and you fully made that decision on your own. Now, I wonder if it was more out of insecurity because you couldn't stand the thought of me being here on my own, living my life, being so independent.

I loved you then, and I love you now.

I hope you're in the mountains facing your demons head on. It wasn't fair they came out to haunt me.

I pray that you find peace. I hope someday you'll see the perfection in it all. That maybe we weren't meant to last a lifetime, but we carried each other through and simultaneously propelled the other one forward to another level, to more self-love and awareness.

I'm grateful for you, and I'm sorry if I forgot to tell you that.

Hatred

He hated them.
He hated them for what they'd done to me.
And he hated that I didn't hate them.

What he never understood was that the hatred I carried all those
years never actually hurt them. It hurt me.

Hatred made me sick.
It made my chest burn.
My back ache.
My immune system weak.

Hatred kept me awake at night.
My jaw clenched.
My fingernails ripped to shreds.

Hatred brought anxiety.
Anxiety brought fear.
Fear brought depression.

So no, I didn't hate them anymore.
I wouldn't give them that power.

I chose to understand.
I chose to forgive.
I chose to find peace.

He loved me so much, he couldn't bear the thought of others
hurting me.
But I never gave him that burden to carry.
I exhausted myself trying to make him see.

And he chose to not understand.

He chose to not forgive.
He chose to not be at peace.

It wasn't really the others he hated.
It was the pieces of himself he recognized in them.

Soak in and feel the magic of this Spotify Playlist I created for
The Lost Boys:

https://open.spotify.com/user/1265771279/playlist/6g3ZhDN69
GRZ0k2Ih2ADsh?si=R5dFjv7SSHqUyw-QHvpbfw

Chapter 3

Raw
&
Real

Raw and Real is all the feels.

These poems, essays and stories are the shadow parts of my journey many times through the Dark Night of the Soul.

We all have a shadow. It's all the dark, heavy thoughts and emotions we don't allow anyone else to see or even want to acknowledge as existing within us. They're the fears, traumas and desires we've repressed.

They're the pieces we keep hidden, and the stories we don't tell.

It's in the hiding of our shadows, however, that we give them power over us. Not until we share our truths can we illuminate what's in the dark.

May you courageously dance with and honor your shadows. And may you come to understand that it's just a stop along the road, not your final destination.

May you find bits and pieces of yourself in my shadow stories and through compassion for yourself, open up to the possibility of emerging from your shadows magically transformed.

Shadows of BDSM

Please Hurt Me
(2015)

Give me that release
Break me down
Make me forget all that is around

Make me cry
Make me gasp
Make me hate you
Then touch me tenderly
Look in my eyes
And hurt me again

Leave me bruised
Beaten
Red
Disheveled

Don't tell me I'm beautiful
Or pretty
Call me a whore
Call me a slut
Play with my mind just enough

Make it okay
To want to hurt
Do this for me
You're the only one who can

Hurt me to take away the pain
The disappointment

The disgust
I will give you all of it
You're the only one I trust

Hit me
Choke me
Leave me breathless
Only then can I slip away unnoticed
And you
Will still be my friend

Step Right Up
(2015)

I bear these marks proudly
The bruises upon my flesh
The scars within my heart
The torment of my mind

Little reminders of the filth
The sickness and darkness
That reside within my soul

I welcome the pain
Deeper and harder each time
Never satisfied
Always longing for more

Counting the minutes
Taking it all
Knowing full well
I will break when I fall

The silence is my friend
It's the company I keep
I strive for it
Crave it
Push myself through anything
To taste that sweet nothingness

I'm cursed with this affliction
The pain is my addiction
Battered, lost, lonely
Walking through these streets

It all becomes a blur

I'm invisible
Which way is home
I battle through the unknown

Dancing with my demons
Torturing myself
Begging for reprieve
Silent cries within this hell

Blood, lust and envy
Old familiar songs
What have I created
It feels so right and yet so wrong

Tipping the scales
Deciding which way to go
Welcoming you all
To this fucked up show

A Storm Rages
(2015)

A storm rages
Hidden beneath the surface
Of pretty things
It's threatening to undo
The threads
Of my established peace

There's a fire burning
Deep inside
It's wild and unkempt
Emotions are swelling
Stirring up
The darkness in my mind
I'm taunted to go there
I'm trying to resist

But if it grabs hold
Take me away from here
Give me the pain that takes
Everything else away

On the Edge
(2015)

Some days I fall flat on my face
Consumed by the things I don't want to face

Some days it's all too much
Emotions bubbling up
Mind a mess
Thoughts frantic

It feels like I'm
Overflowing my cup
I just can't do it
I say in my head
As I struggle to get myself out of bed

But piece by piece
And limb by limb
I summon the strength
I carry deep within

I won't let the shadow side
Take control this time
No matter how many nights
I come home and cry

It's my job to solve the problems
It's on me to figure this all out
And occasionally
I sit atop a mountain of doubt

So please take it away
Run your fingers down my back
Give my ass a hard smack

Wrap me up tight
So I cannot move
Push me hard
I've got something to prove

Put your hands around my neck
In such a loving embrace
Notice the calm
That comes over my face

Do not give me
The option to breathe
It's only then
I will trust you
I need to believe

Wash away the pain
By making me hurt
Slide your fingers up my thighs
Feel the wetness
Beneath my skirt

Tears they will fall
As I struggle to escape it all

Beneath the surface
Just waiting to erupt
Take it all away
I need to feel like I'm enough

Take my power
Some days I have too much
I don't want all this control
All this responsibility and such

Offer me release

From this jaded mind
Bruise me, abuse me
Lose all sense of time

Let me escape into you
For just one night
So I may wake up in the morning
Ready and willing
To conquer this fight

At War
(2015)

I was foolish to believe
You would take what I'm offering

My mind is at war with my heart
My heart wants you to tear my body apart

These questions in my head
Kept me up all night in my bed
Feeling all alone
So desperate for a home

When did you start to care
And why
Why can't I have it all?

I thought I had it straight
But as usual I'm divided

All these new ideas, new concepts
Get my head spinning
I want to break free of what's normal

I want to run far, far away
But it's just this battle in my mind
That won't quiet down

I might even tell you
If you were still around

Shadows of Abuse

Look at you
(2016)

*"Look at you. Nobody else will ever want you. You're nothing.
You're just a pathetic, horrible person."*

He took those words and like daggers, stabbed me in the heart.
I'm not sure what triggered him that day.

He knew I was unhappy. I'd brought my daughter back from El
Salvador eight months earlier than expected when gunshots
outside our front door became a regular occurrence. He had to
wait it out, anticipating the arrival of his visa any day, so he
could return to the States.

When he finally came back, it was a joyous reunion. I'd already
spent four years in the immigration system, which was a living
hell to begin with. But his return meant I'd done something right,
and it was a relief to feel needed and wanted.

But during our months apart, something in him had changed.
While he'd been gone, I kept having this feeling that something
was off, even though he assured me everything was okay. The
days we didn't talk were due to "power outages and sketchy wifi", even though we both knew that I knew the truth.

He always had a short fuse. And this particular day, something
set him off. He could feel me pulling away, perhaps, starting to
daydream about a life without him. And there was no way he
was going to stand for that.

And then again, he said:

"Look at you. Nobody else will ever want you. You're nothing. You're just a pathetic, horrible person."

I didn't have the strength to fight back, or the confidence to believe anything different about myself. And in that moment, I was frightened as he reminded me of my father.

He stood in my face in the hallway, facing the bedroom, spewing his venom. His stature grew bigger, and my self-worth was hanging by a thread.

We moved to the kitchen, where dishes were thrown in my direction, with the baby crying, as I begged him to relent. Broken plates and bowls smashed against the wall, and then fell to the floor. I held my daughter to keep her out of harm's way, and he stopped. Then he walked over and said:

Clean it up.
You're nothing. Nobody could ever want you. Just look at you now.

The Dimming
(2017)

It was when I felt my light starting to dim again that I made the shift. It wasn't a huge proclamation, but a subtle shift within me. My self-worth had been nagging at me because it had been cast aside.

The dimming wasn't straight away but happened slowly over time, as it always did with him. And before I knew it, I hardly recognized myself anymore.

In those moments, you start to question yourself. You wonder where that confident girl from even two weeks ago went. Welcoming him back into my life and my body was a poetic dance of bliss and destruction.

I still have yet to discover how one man can strip me of all my dignity, self-worth and self-respect, and in such a pragmatic way.

But this time, my inner voice cried out. This time I thought of Iceland. I thought about how much I'd accomplished and how much I deserved.

Why was it so hard for me to really believe that?
Why do I go back over and over to the dog that bites me?

You want to have your cake and eat it, too. That's why.

The Rape
(2016)

My anger boils up around me
Like your hands on my throat
I want to scream
But I can't

Your palms muffle the sounds
You pull from the root
My hair between your fingers
I kick, I writhe
I feel you between my thighs

I want you off
I want you gone
I want to forget all I've done wrong

You laugh in my face
As if this were a joke
You squeeze tighter and tighter
As I begin to choke

Desperate for air
Begging for strength
My mind spinning
You are everything that's wrong in this world
And me?
Well I'm just a scared little girl

I thought I had it under control
I thought I had you figured out
My mistake was going to that house

I ignored my gut

I don't like to disappoint
But I'm not your plaything
I'm not a body for you to use
You don't get to make decisions for me
I'm the one who gets to choose

Shadows of Divorce

There's No Time For a Breakdown
(2015)

There's no time for a breakdown, babygirl
Pull yourself together
There's too much to do
There's no time

Nobody's going to save you, babygirl
There's only you
Dry those eyes
Get your head on straight
There's bills to pay
A child to raise
And you can't look disheveled
For your date

There's no time for a breakdown, babygirl
Don't let her see
You've shed too many tears

Show her you're strong, babygirl
Prove them all wrong

You have to go back inside now, babygirl
It's not safe for you to play
The world is too cold and you can't stay
Mama's got this handled, babygirl
I have a plan
But you have to stay inside
Until it's safe again

There's no time for a breakdown, babygirl
Put on that beautiful smile
Just get through this day
It will all be worthwhile
I promise

The Storm
(2015)

Her inadequacies trickle down
Like raindrops on the window
They pool up around her
Like the flood from last night's storm

Lightning strikes her heart
She gets frightened
Chaos stirs up
As she runs inside for shelter

She hides in the corner
In the dark recesses of her mind
Wondering how many hours or days or weeks
The storm will last this time

Can we skip the weekend?
(2015)

There's a fine line
between pleasure and pain
They wash over
As if they are one in the same

Happiness and sorrow
Feelings you can't escape
Moments I wish to have back
Grief of knowing there's memories
I can no longer make

Each holiday
Every birthday
All the so called important dates
Make it harder to live with
the countless mistakes

My Year of Firsts
(2015)

One year ago today, I drove home from a friend's birthday party. I cried the entire way. I walked into my house, went up to our room and sat on the bed. He came up and asked what was wrong. I told him I was done, and I was leaving. The next day I packed my stuff, took our daughter and left.

Most days I have no regrets. Most days I'm happier than I've ever been. I'm becoming the person I've always wanted to be. The person I knew I was destined to become.

I cherish my time with my daughter above all else and those are my best days. Most days I push through for her and some have even become effortless. Most days I see all that's good in my life. I see how far I've come in the past year, and I'm hopeful for the future.

That's most days.

Then there's the other days.

Days where I'll be getting ready in the morning and, in a split second, I'm on the bathroom floor, crying. Days where I miss our family unit. Days where I think about all the ways he's replaced me with his now live-in girlfriend and how much my daughter loves her, and it breaks my heart.

I think about how they're now a happy family unit, and I blame myself because I left. There are times I want to scream and cry and lash out. Some days I feel self-destructive, and I just don't care. Some days just feel off. (This week has felt off.)

I knew this weekend was coming. I knew when the months changed from July to August. This week I've cried every day, sometimes out of nowhere. This week my mind has been playing tricks on me.

He lashed out on me last week, and I haven't fully recovered. I try to hide the pain his words cause and the damage he does. It reminds me why I left. It reminds me why I planned my escape for two years. But that doesn't lessen the grief or the beating that my self-esteem takes.

I ran into a friend at the store last night. When I told her this is *the* weekend she jumped for joy. She reminded me I've gotten through all "the firsts." All the birthdays, anniversaries, holidays, etc. I've gotten through all of them, and those are the hardest. That gave me hope. But today I'm still grieving, and my heart hurts and my makeup is running.

I'm heading out to meet my friend for lunch. The one who's house I left that fateful night. The one who took in my daughter and I for four months when I left, because my family turned their backs, and I had nowhere to go. It will be good to see her, but the memories are flooding in, and I just pray I make it through this weekend. My last weekend of "firsts."

Lost
(2015)

I've lost myself
In the chaos and lack of magic in the world
No inspiration to write
Not a picture taken

I've drifted off
Into a quiet restlessness
I've been overwhelmed by the things
That make us human

Responsibilities have weighed me down
And the only voice I have
Is the incessant chatter in my head

I want to feel the magic again
The energy of the moon almost did me in
I was awake the whole night
In his bed

I'm terrified of this world
That each day sucks the life right out of me
When all I want to do is love
Be loved and cared for

My solitude has brought about a peace
And yet a lonely ache in my heart
As I yearn for balance
And I crave to understand the lesson
That perhaps I will never learn
Because it's not about an end goal

One of those days
(2015)

Today's one of those days.

I had a family day with my parents, brother and nephew. We took my daughter to the pumpkin patch. It was a "good" day, I guess. But it was one of those days I hated being the single mom amidst a sea of families. It's not even rational as I had my whole family around me, but I just felt off.

My ex-husband and his girlfriend moved into their new house this weekend. They conveniently just had to move right down the street from one of my best friends and her daughter.

We went to their house yesterday and saw it all. We saw the moving truck, the boxes, the girlfriend in the window unpacking. It was perfect. The perfect, fucking cute little house.

Up until that moment I hadn't cared. It really didn't seem to be bothering me too much that he was getting a house with her and his kids. But when I drove by, my heart felt like it might explode. If my little one hadn't been in the car, I could've screamed. But she was there, and the feelings have been festering ever since.

Today's just one of those days.

I made a delicious dinner tonight. It came out of nowhere. I hadn't even planned it, but I did my weekly meal-prepping while I cooked as well. Cooking makes me happy, but I finished and just felt sad.

It's one of those days I wish I had someone to share this meal with. Those days I wish someone would ask me how my day was and just put their arms around me. Those days when I wish I didn't have to be strong.

Tomorrow starts my first day of going full-time with my job. I'm super-excited and have appointments booked all week, but I think the reality of what I'm about to create is hitting me. Although it's all great and wonderful, I'm feeling overwhelmed already. And I wish I had someone who believes in me and would tell me it's all going to be great.

Growing up, I always secretly dreamed of becoming a single mom. *Who the fuck actually wants to be a single mom?!* Maybe it was because I idolized my mom and, even though she fucked up a lot, she never gave up. She was the best, badass single mom.

Maybe it's because I'm a control freak and wanted to raise my daughter the way I wanted. I'm not sure why I always wished it upon myself, but I certainly got what I asked for.

I love my life. I love being single. I love the journey. The self-discovery. I love my freedom. And I love my daughter.

But today is just one of those days.

Take it away
(2015)

It's a dull ache
The kind that can go unnoticed
It's not the type that breaks you
But it slowly creeps in the crevices in your heart

It's the heaviness
That makes you hide in the bathroom
When you're surrounded by loved ones

It's not the kind of sadness that has you crying yourself to sleep
at night
But it lingers in the air
Knowing not everything is right

It's the tightness in the chest
It's the panic that threatens your sanity
It's staring in the mirror
And questioning everything

It's feeling alone
So very alone
In your thoughts
The irrational emotions
Not being able to separate the truth from fiction

Wondering why
Attempting to figure out what it means
What's the purpose?
What's the lesson this time?
Please just show me a sign

Take it away

Please leave me be
I'm tired of suffering this drawn out misery

The Darkness
(2015)

I've always enjoyed being alone.

I don't mind going to movies by myself, getting coffee alone or even going to dinner for one. In the summer, I can spend hours hiking, swimming and laying on the beach by myself. And most of the time, I don't even mind going to bed every night alone.

I genuinely enjoy my own company, and I'm not afraid of who I am when I'm alone. It's in these times when I discover who I am and can get in touch with the beautiful stillness of life.

I've come to terms with and accepted most of the various parts of *Kelsey*. Still working on some, as I'm always a work in progress, but for the most part, I understand what I'm dealing with. The beautiful, the ugly. The hot and cold. The light and the dark and so forth.

I rarely get alone time, so, when I do, I bask in the silence.

But then there are the other times. I can usually feel when those times are coming. I can have a great day, feeling happy, with things going along just fine. I'll be out all day and then go home, letting the time slip by, doing a whole lot of nothing. And then I get anxious. And in my anxiousness, I'm not quite sure what it is I want. I'm exhausted beyond belief and, yet, I can't wind down. I decide I need to get out, but then I don't have the energy to get ready or figure out what I want to do and with whom. It's these times I don't want to be alone.

It's a bizarre feeling that only gets stronger as the night moves on. When the sun is up, I can stay perky. I can stay my happy, content self. I can distract myself by life. But then the sun goes down, and the darkness comes. And with the darkness comes loneliness. And it's the kind of loneliness that makes your stomach hurt. That deep, dark hole. I don't cry. I'm not even angry. I'm totally void of emotion. And it doesn't feel like there's anything to fill the hole. I just sit in the silence.

Music isn't even comforting. Nothing is comforting. My thoughts are even somewhat still.

It's these moments that I don't want to be alone. I want someone's arms around me, just holding me. I want to feel loved and have someone pet me while I fall asleep and then hold me through the night.

I want someone on my side, so I don't have to go through everything alone. I want to tell someone about my day while I sit here on the bed in my pajamas with no makeup and just out of the shower (when I feel my most beautiful). And I want someone to tell me it's all going to be alright even though I already know it is. I want to matter to someone, and I desperately need someone to make me laugh.

These are the darkest nights. Sometimes, I can snap out of it quickly and get myself in check, but other times, the darkness consumes me. Sometimes, I even want to be consumed.

The Feels
(2015)

Curled up
Blankies tucked in securely
Eyes closed
Attempting to escape me
It's not working
Fuck I need a drink
But I'm not doing that anymore
Fuck I need a cigarette
Too bad I don't smoke
I need endless orgasms
But of course, I'm on my period
So I lay here
Ignoring my to-do list
Nothing new
Dishes piling
Laundry all over the floor
Baby calls me crying
She misses me
I curl up a little more snug
I scratch at my head
I really want to claw
But it doesn't make the voices go away
And my body still aches
And I'm tired
So fucking tired
I tell myself to get up
Indecision
Indifference
Numb
And yet feeling everything

"Having anxiety and depression is like being scared and tired at the same time. It's the fear of failure, but no urge to be productive. It's wanting friends, but hate socializing. It's wanting to be alone, but not wanting to be lonely. It's caring about everything then caring about nothing. It's feeling everything at once then feeling paralyzingly numb." - Author unknown

Dark Days
(2015)

Worthless
Horrible
Whore
You're not special

Why would anyone want to be with you?
You're nothing
I can't stand you
How could anyone else?
What the fuck is wrong with you?

On my dark days his voice still haunts me
Sharp little cuts like a razor blade
His words echo in my head
As I try to shake them away

On my dark days I believe him
One moment of weakness is all it takes
These days I feel myself crumbling
Seven years of harsh words
Not so easy to forget
In the end I never slept

Awoken each night to a nightmare
Berating and then raping
Tears streaming while I held the pillow between my teeth

The perfect couple in public
The screams in the car on the drive home
I was never enough
On my dark days I will never be enough

Slut. Terrible mother. Selfish.
You never think of her because you're too busy out fucking
around
You asked for this
You chose this

His harsh words have continued long after the end
I thought leaving would save her
But every Tuesday I drop her off at counseling
And I wonder if all I've done is fuck her up

On my dark days I don't feel strong
On these days all I see is everything I've done wrong
Solitude is my only escape
Nestled on the couch with my demons
Unsure how long they will stick around this time

On my dark days I need the pain
Hurt me until I can shut off my brain

You're still the love of my life
Why did you do this?
I still think about you all the time
I miss you
These are his words and they cut just as much

The mind-fuck
His favorite game
Drunken late-night calls

I look forward to the day I wake up and his words cease to
bother me
Maybe the whispers in my ear will no longer evoke my worst
fears

Shadows of Heartbreak

I wish it was you
(2016)

When they call
I wish it was you

When they text
I hope to see your name

When they're talking to me
I wonder what you'd be saying

When they want to see me
I wonder why you don't

When I'm fucking them
Your face flashes through my mind

When I'm pretending with them
I wish I could just be real
With you

Sleepy thoughts aren't rational
(2016)

It's in the darkness
That I miss you
The cold silence of this room
I don't cry for you anymore
But sometimes my heart feels so heavy without knowing what's
to come

I'm happy in my solitude
Loneliness is no longer my friend
I've said goodbye to the comfortable sadness
I've become content

But then at night
When I'm tired
So very tired
I miss you
I long to hear your voice

You're just a ghost
I've created in my mind
Addicted to you I remain
Even after everything has changed

So easily I can let go
But not of you
You're stuck to me like glue

I told you today you'd be my ultimate hate fuck
Hating you and loving you
It all feels the same
I'd give anything to hear you say my name

I'll drift off to sleep once again
And I'll be freed from these complicated chains you keep me in

Betrayal
(April 25, 2017)

The betrayal runs deep and thick today.
I'm desperate for answers.
For a truth I will never get.

What is truth?
I suppose that's all relative anyway.
But I want to know how exactly how far back the betrayal goes.
I'm trying to justify things.
I met his mother.
We spent time with our kids.

And all the while, I knew it wasn't right.
Not only did he betray me,
But the ultimate betrayal was to myself.

Before
(2017)

Before the ugliness
I was your woman
And you were my man

Before the bitterness
I was your princess
You were my king

Before the emptiness
I was your muse
Now I sit in silence
And write about only you

Shadows of Sex Work

Let Me Forget
(2016)

I sit here in this hotel room
So many thoughts
So many unanswered questions

Questions of the heart
Questions of life

Most days I know my purpose
Most days I'm full of hope

Other days I'm lost
This day I'm lost

Memories of what happened in this room haunt me
Not even twelve hours ago

The rush
And then the despair
And yet I came back here
To escape the horrors in my heart
To be at peace with who I am
And the things I do

I can only pray my mind will settle down
That I won't drown in this leftover champagne

That I can see the light I left on
In the darkness

That the morning sun
Will make me remember how much I shine
And that life won't be like this forever

Soak in and feel the magic of this Spotify Playlist I created for
Raw & Real:

https://open.spotify.com/user/1265771279/playlist/4vcgPiiiNHu
QLQN7MSbWTF?si=oOiXplqzSoyxWbSAyPoBlw

Chapter 4

Healing My Heart

Healing is a journey. It's the part of the path where you begin to dance with forgiveness, acceptance and clarity. It's a constant opening and closing, expansion and contraction.

It's where you start to feel safe again. And just as you begin to open and blossom, you quickly close right back up and retreat.

It's the uncharted territory of the space that's created when you let someone or something go. It's surrendering to the sweet in-between. The place where you're no longer who you were, but you aren't quite yet who you long to be.

Here's what it's looked and felt like for me…

One More Day
(2015)

You can do it, baby girl
Just one more day
Breathe through the tears
Fight through the pain
Just get through today

Get yourself out of bed
Put on some clothes
Clean the house
Make your to-do list
Focus
Just one more day

Don't worry about yesterday
Don't wonder about tomorrow
There's someone counting on you
Baby girl, it's going to be okay
If you can just make it through a few more hours

The hurt might not go away
Your chest may still feel heavy
The thoughts will spin
But if you can get through to the end
You will have won
Just for today

Movin on up!
(2015)

Ten months ago, I told my husband I was leaving for good this time. The next morning, while he was at work, I packed my bags and took our 6-year-old daughter and moved across town to stay with a friend in her tiny loft apartment. I had no car, no home and $50 to my name.

Things were rough, to say the least. I went through the darkest period of my life, and it still gives me chills to think of myself lying on the floor of my bedroom for days on end, physically immobile and sobbing my eyes out. My daughter witnessed the whole thing. That brought more shame than anything. I'm very close with my family, but they were so upset they wouldn't even speak to me for weeks.

I was a mess and couldn't even function to get a job. I was driving one of my ex's cars and, in the midst of my depression, thinking things couldn't get worse, the car was stolen from in front of the apartment, driven to a nearby town and set on fire. Seriously, WTF?! It was bizarre, a scene out of a movie, and it was my breaking point.

In the midst of all this, I was introduced to kink and was being beaten (consensually) and manipulated (not consensual) by someone very inexperienced in the community. Hot mess doesn't begin to describe me.

I stayed with my friend for four months before my parents finally offered to my daughter and me to stay with them. Reluctantly, I agreed so I could get my shit together. I moved in the week of Thanksgiving while they went away and took my daughter with them on holiday. (I still dislike any and all holidays.)

In January, I finally figured out a career path and got three jobs to save up the money for a trip to Atlanta to get a certification in my new field. I busted my ass. Not many people believed in me. Only a select few thought I would actually achieve my goal. After I accomplished that goal in March, I cried for a week straight, and it was one of the proudest moments of my life.

Since then, I started my new job, and it's something I'm super-duper passionate about and wouldn't change for anything. I actually love going to work. Not many people can say that.

Living with my parents isn't something I tell anyone. There's only a handful of people who know that's where I've been living. Frankly, it's nobody's damn business where I live. But even though it was necessary and got me to where I am, it's something I've been ashamed to tell people.

Soooo, my big news of the day is that after the ten most intense months of my life, I just got the keys to my very own apartment! This is a huge deal for me, and I just want to start sobbing in a good way, but I can't, because I already did my makeup, and I'm heading out to a concert. Lol. I'm in shock, and I'm super-overwhelmed and proud of myself.

I haven't lived on my own and been responsible for all my own bills in eight years! It's kinda scary, especially since now I have a little one. too, but I've never been so glad to give someone such a big chunk of money! Things will be tight for a while, and I'm sure I will stress every day about making sure I can do it, but I have done it so far and will continue to take it one day at a time.

Today, I just want to bask in this feeling and then, tomorrow, I get to start moving! Telling my daughter we were moving was, again, one of the proudest moments of my life. I often feel like a failure as a mother, but I'm going to be the one to show her that you can accomplish anything you set your mind to. It may not always be pretty or how you want it to look, but with each setback, you only get stronger.

A New Day
(2015)

Today was a new day

Today I wasn't a victim
A victim of circumstance
Or of someone else's actions

Today I didn't feel torn down
Or ashamed
I wasn't belittled
And I didn't play games

Today the sun shone on my face
I found my strength once again
I remembered how far I've come
In the darkness, I wouldn't remain

Today I found the girl
The one who doesn't take shit
The one who sees every obstacle
And rides the waves

Today I found the woman
Who gets up every day
Despite endless challenges
Never-ending frustrations and setbacks
She keeps a smile on her face
She's the one who will inspire you
The one who will always care for you
She won't let her heart grow cold

With each heartache, she learns
And she grows stronger from it

She won't be defeated

With each person that leaves her life
She can see the perfection
And she's grateful for the knowledge

Today I found me
I may not remember tomorrow
But just for today
I discovered a new way

It's not you, It's me
(2015)

I had one of those mind-blowing, aha, light bulb moments today. I was driving home from the gym, which always stirs up lots of energy. I was being very introspective, thinking about my past two failed relationships and what it is about these two men that makes me completely bonkers, wondering why I just can't seem to let go of my emotional attachment to either of them.

I was thinking about all the things they both did that made me so unhappy. And as usual, I was getting all into the very hurtful things they did and said to me repeatedly and how I reacted to those things. And I was getting annoyed that I keep replaying this same story over and over.

And then it hit me! It hit me hard!

I keep telling myself I need to let those things go, move on and forgive them. But why can't I seem to do it?

And then the missing piece appeared...I have to FORGIVE MYSELF!

When I think back to the person I was in my marriage, I'm ashamed. I'm ashamed of the person I became over the course of six years. It wasn't me. To everyone else, I was myself – happy, positive and cheerful. But, within the walls of my home, I was a very dark, angry person.

Our relationship was volatile and full of hurt and anguish. I hated who I was within our family dynamic. Many events led to us being that way, but the fact of the matter was, I wasn't me.

I can blame the years of verbal and emotional abuse, I can blame the broken dishes and holes in the wall, I can blame the months of being raped by my own husband. There's still a lot I need to forgive. But most of all, I realized I need to forgive myself and the person I was at that time.

Then came my first kink relationship, only weeks after the ending of my marriage. This is a biggie. This is the one that still makes me cry. I haven't known why I just can't move past the emotions of it, and I judge myself very harshly for letting it still get to me. But the aha came today when realizing I absolutely despise myself for who I was in that dynamic as well. I don't like her one bit.

That was a very broken, very vulnerable little girl. She cried every day, all day, about everything. She was weak. She was needy. She was jealous and possessive. And she became insecure in the worst of ways. She was beaten down by mind games and felt helpless and let someone else control her.

These are all the things I despise.

I get physically ill thinking about who I was at that time. It was the furthest from myself and my truth that I have ever been in my life.

So, when I realized this today, it became crystal clear and a weight was lifted. I may not be ready to forgive them for their hurtful actions and hurtful words, but I can forgive myself.

I CAN decide not to hate those parts of me or who I was during those times.

I CAN recognize that I was doing the best I possibly could at the time, in those circumstances.

I CAN forgive that little girl and that monster.

I CAN move on, knowing I'm happier than I've ever been, more confident in myself than I've ever been.

I still have my demons and that little girl is still in there, but it's okay.

I CAN love every part of me…because it is me.

And that's what I feel like I'm doing within this lifestyle. I'm discovering and uncovering parts of myself I didn't even know I needed to see and others I had no idea were even there. And I'm loving this person I've always been and was always meant to be.

For the first time in my life, I feel like I can just be me.

Sometimes, it feels like without the caffeine, alcohol and sugar, I've been split wide open. I'm like a nasty open wound, bleeding all over the place. And I don't know how to sew myself up.

I keep asking myself how I got to this place in my life.

At what point did things start to fall apart?

How did I get here, and how do I get out of here?

Will I ever stop struggling?

Will I ever wake up in the morning without wishing I hadn't?

Will the anxiety and panic attacks ever stop?

I'm tired. Just so fucking tired.

My baby girl is struggling and, more than anything, it breaks my heart a little more each day. So, each morning I get up and think of her. I relish in my time with her. I love making her breakfast, packing her lunch and driving her to school. She needs me more than ever right now and, for the first time in a long time, I see how much I need her, too.

Dear Little Me
(2015)

It wasn't your fault, honey. None of it was ever your fault. You're too young to see what you saw, to feel how you feel. Your innocence was taken too soon and, unfortunately, those memories will haunt you forever. But please, I beg you, don't ever blame yourself.

You've already taken on a burden that isn't yours to carry. Put it down now. Don't let the weight crush you. You're so young and sweet and have such a big heart.

People will tell you that you feel too much. Sometimes, you might even believe that because you're special, little one. You can see what no one else sees. That does not make you crazy. Don't ever let anyone make you believe you're crazy.

You stay quiet and shy because you feel everything around you, and you don't know what to do with that. It makes you feel isolated, but please don't hide.

You're not alone. You were never alone and never will be alone. Sometimes the journey is lonely, but when you love yourself unconditionally, nothing else matters. But you have to reach out. You will encounter some beautiful souls in your life. Let them in. They will be a calm place.

Your smile lights up a room, and your personality will win over most. Never hold back the amazing person you will become.

Stay close with your siblings or, one day, you'll wake up and realize it's been over a year since you spoke to them, and your heart will hurt. Let go of the resentments and betrayals of your family. In the end, even if they've turned their backs, it was out of love, and they'll truly be the ones who have your back.

Be gentle, little one. You were brought to this Earth to do amazing things. Love with all your heart. Be true to yourself always, and your light will shine so bright you'll help guide the way for others out of the darkness. You're a natural healer, my child. Utilize those gifts while you're still young. The world needs people like you, and you're loved beyond belief!

Grief Isn't Linear
(2015)

Some days it comes out of nowhere…the grief. Seemingly normal activities serve as keys that unlock the messy, broken pieces of our hearts.

I was surprised when I found myself excited about Christmas this year. I really thought I'd lost all of my holiday cheer years ago during the decline of our marriage. I was thrilled when I picked up the little one from her dad's so I could tell her we were going to put up the tree over the weekend. Then, she told me how they had already done it. And my heart sank.

Last Christmas, I was in mourning because he'd told me he'd thrown away all my Christmas decorations, things I'd had for years in my family. I hated him and vowed to never forgive him.

When I moved into my apartment in the spring, he dropped off the remains of my stuff, which included everything he'd said he'd thrown away. *Asshole.*

Over the weekend, I continued with my plan of decorating. We put up the tree, just the two of us. I decided halfway through that I hated most of the ornaments, the ones he and I had bought together. So, the little one and I bought new ones and hung them up, making that tree our own.

I found myself crying throughout the day, here and there. Little tears would quietly stream down my face as I unpacked everything, trying my best to hide it from her. I'd been so excited with the whole tree decorating bullshit that, I didn't expect myself to get so emotional. But there it was.

● ● ●

Tomorrow marks 7 years since my daughter was born. Tonight, we made cookies for her to take to school in the morning. But, we got in a fight before bed. It had been a long day, she was tired, I hadn't eaten all day. (I was barely sleeping anymore, either.) She went to bed mad at me. I told her I was going out to the kitchen to eat.

I barely made it out of the room before I found myself sobbing on the kitchen floor. I'd just told her the story of when she was born. It was the most amazing, magical day of my life. It was perfection. I cried for three days straight, overwhelmed by the amount of love one could feel for another human being.

As I cried, I stared at that tree, we'd bought it the year she was born. We used to lay her underneath it, and she'd stare at the lights. I'm so grateful to still have it, but it also pulls at my heartstrings.

I've spent the last two days trying to find her the "perfect" present. Turns out, it doesn't exist.

Seriously, I have close to zero free time, but every time I had a few minutes between clients at work I'd run to the store. In the end, I failed. I didn't get anything spectacular, and she wasn't overjoyed.

What I realized is that I was acting like a crazy person about a damn present. But why?

Because I compare myself to them. His party will be better, his gifts will be more elaborate and more expensive, most likely exactly what she wants. The girlfriend will bake her a cake, her siblings will give her all the attention a girl could need.

And then there's me. Just over here alone. Doing everything my goddamn self, trying so hard to make her birthday special.

● ● ●

Lately, she wants me to be everywhere, all the time. I keep telling her I'm just one person, just one. It's only me. I don't have a partner to play house with. I don't have teenage kids to clean my house. Nobody else makes her breakfast, brushes her teeth and hair. Nobody else packs her lunch and drives her to school. It's just me. I'm not them.

When I get overwhelmed, I try to explain this to her. It's not her fault, but she gets caught in my grumpiness, more often than not. So tonight, I'm overwhelmed. I'm overwhelmed with work, with life, with this single mom bullshit. And tonight, I'm grieving.

I used to think grieving was this thing I was going through and then, one day, it would end. It doesn't happen like that. Grief isn't linear.

I don't have days like this very often anymore. Compared to where I was even a few months ago, I hardly even cry. I want to judge myself and think I'm going backwards, as if I'm not supposed to have emotions anymore. But that's not how these things work and, tonight, I have a lot of stupid emotions.

• • •

7. She's turning 7. I was 7 when my parents divorced and broke my heart. Each day I wake up, my goal is to keep her heart intact.

"Grief never ends...but it changes. It's a passage, not a place to stay. Grief is not a sign of weakness, nor a lack of faith...it is the price of love." --- Author Unknown

Thoughts on Letting Go
(2015)

Letting go has always been a struggle for me. I'll hold onto people for dear life. If you're important to me in any way, letting you go will not be an easy task.

Unfortunately, relationships shift and evolve, for better or worse. This goes for any type of dynamic, be it friends or lovers. In the end, it's always the same. The struggle to let go is real.

I notice I go through a set of emotions with the ending of relationships. There's a pattern I recognize, which almost makes this whole "breaking up" with people thing a little easier because now I know what to expect from myself.

At first, I get very sad. The loss of a friend or lover is a low blow, and I grieve and mourn the ending...until...I don't anymore. I get depressed and sad. I think of all the happy times that will never come again and the future that won't come at all. I cry and cry. And go to the gym...a lot.

Then I get angry. I hate the other person. I think of all their flaws and all the things wrong with them. I remember all the things they did to hurt/upset me, and I want to smash their face in the pavement. Then I go to the gym...a lot.

The anger, rage and sadness all take turns, weighing heavily on my heart and head, threatening my peace of mind that I've worked so hard for.

Then there's a shift at some point, and I start to really look deep inside of myself. I question why I'm reacting so harshly, what I can do to remedy the situation, and I look at what I need to do to create peace in my life again.

Ultimately, nobody can make us feel any certain way. My emotions are on me, and they aren't anyone else's responsibility. This is easy to say but not so easy to remember.

So, I use the "breakup" as a growth opportunity. I get real with myself. I start to build my confidence back up. I take action.

I remind myself there's nothing wrong with me. I'm not too much or not enough…for anyone. I'm me, perfect the way I am.

People come and go. I've grown accustomed to it. I switched schools almost every year of my life and spent most of my adult life traveling. But one thing that has never gotten easier is letting go. I still grieve. I'm still human. If you're one of the lucky ones, I get attached to you.

One thing I do know though is that when I'm done, I'm done. And when I finally reach that point, there's usually no turning back. I will never emotionally invest in you again. The chord finally is cut. But that ending doesn't come without a fight.

My heart is vast and full, and if I let you into it, and you hurt me, I will leave claw marks upon your exit from my life.

Forgotten Dreams
(2015)

There's something that happens to a woman when she's gotten everything she ever wanted, only to watch her life crumble around her. When the future you'd planned in your head is ripped to shreds in one single, solitary moment. Hopes, dreams, goals become a distant memory. Goals become much more mundane. Life becomes about survival.

Every single mom I know can understand this feeling, and these women have become my refuge. It's their humility, strength and power that makes these women beautiful.

I've always had a wild spirit. I've never stayed in any one place very long. I never wanted to be a housewife. Even when I was a housewife, I always had outside ventures.

I've always been an entrepreneur. I've always been ambitious and wanted more out of life. I'm the type to have lists, lots of lists. I've made dream boards and goal sheets. I've sat in meditation and practiced visualization. I've always been a positive type even in times of adversity.

When I left my marriage almost a year ago, I hit rock bottom. I thought I'd been there before, but in this black pit of despair, I discovered a new level of darkness and emptiness. Every big dream or goal I ever had was forgotten, lost in the depths of anxiety and depression.

I couldn't function at all for the first three months. I had no motivation, no ambition, no desire, except to drink and fuck and forget the pain. Around month five, I suddenly gained some smidgen of clarity and discovered the career path I'd always wanted. I was finally able to work again and lost myself in being busy. I was able to set a few goals and was proud when I reached them. But the majority of these goals were still basics of survival – feeding my daughter and putting gas in the car.

It was around month nine, my desperation to get my own place and stand on my own two feet trumped any other goals and that became my priority. I did anything and everything I could for money, things I've only shared with a few people and, yet, have since learned are not all that uncommon. Things only a woman in desperate times could understand.

And then I reached my goal. When I got my own place, life changed dramatically. I finally felt like life had a purpose again.

At the moment, life is still about survival, but these past two months, being completely on my own, I've learned more about myself than ever. I've learned how much I can handle in every possible way. I've learned that I'm strong and capable of doing anything. The list of things I've learned could go on for days, and I'm still in the process of discovery.

This morning I woke up and started daydreaming. I was thinking about the trip to Europe I've always wanted to take, and I started planning it in my head. It was fun to entertain for a few minutes. Then, while I was at the gym an hour later, something occurred to me. I had been dreaming! This was huge! It may not sound significant, but it was in every way, and I could feel the shift that had occurred inside me.

For the first time in almost a year, I was dreaming again. I believe that things are getting better, that I'm getting better. I'm finally able to not only focus on what I need to accomplish now, but I'm making lists again. I have a goal sheet, and I've even started checking things off!

My little fantasy of a European trip made me realize just how powerful I am again. Even when things feel stuck, even when I go into my dark places for a few days, or when my emotions wash over me, I always come out ahead. And I can't wait until I take that trip someday!

Thinking about those days when I was lost still takes the air out of my lungs. It still puts knots in my stomach. I don't wish those days on anyone.

(Side Note: Three years later, my European dream came true!)

Her Voice
(2016)

The love was lost
There was nothing to be done
Her heart was gone
He knew he'd done her wrong

She ached for a better life
One he couldn't provide
Each day and night she thought of him and cried
How did their love go astray
She thought about it every day
She dreamed about happier times
But they only existed inside her mind

Now her heart clenches
Her stomach in knots
When she thinks of him
And the love that got lost

Emotions run wild
Words spoken from anger
Never before has she felt in danger
Of her livelihood being stripped away

She gets up and fights
Every single day

She's happier than ever
And now he knows
So every chance he gets
He digs in the low blows

He will get what's coming

Because she's a fighter
She will no longer live under his grip growing tighter

She's taking what's hers
You'd better mark her word
Because never again
Will she allow her voice to go unheard

Seeing the Perfection
(2016)

I'm having one of those moments.

The ones where I see how everything that has happened over the past year has all been in perfect timing, bringing me to where I am now.

I see the perfection in all my experiences and have a calm clarity. And suddenly, I'm grateful for every single one. The good, the bad, the happy and sad.

I'm grateful for the men and the broken hearts and for the people I've met along the way.

My life is about to change in a very exciting way. And I never would have been ready for it if I hadn't gone through all I have. It's all been preparing me for this.

Loss
(2017)

His affections were not because he adored me.
They were because he needed to be adored.

It wasn't the loss of him I grieved.
It was the grief of who I no longer was or would be without him.

Celebration
(July 2017 at Qoya Teacher Training in New Mexico)

Today's theme is celebration.

Not only is it my birthday week, but I'm celebrating and acknowledging the hard work I've put into my life up until now.

I'm celebrating letting go of the past, honoring the present and hope for the future.

I'm celebrating moving out of the darkness and moving forward into the light.

Tears
(2018)

Let those tears fall, my love.
Let them drop so big, they'll fill up an ocean.

Cry it out.
The pain.
The anguish.
The hurt.
Betrayal.

Let it all seep out.
Then let it pour.

Let's make mountains of our grief.
Wrap it around like a warm blanket.
Hold it close, as if your life depends on it.
Because it does.

This is for…
(2019)

All the times I gave my power away

All the times I had sex with tears streaming down my face

The time she said I was just the ugly duckling

The times you told me I was so horrible, nobody else would ever want me

That time you called me a fucking idiot

The times I took on your demons

For the times I shouldered your stress

Missing You
(2019)

It's when I'm happy that I miss you.
Like I want to share it with someone.
I love how your face would light up when you'd see me smile.
Now you hate me.

Dear Kelsey,
(2019)

I know you feel like you should not be thinking about *him*, but I
want you to know it's okay.
I forgive you for feeling guilty and ashamed.
There's nothing wrong with you.

I forgive you for every time you felt less than or not enough.
You are more than enough.
You are magnificent.

I forgive you for all the times you didn't trust yourself.
I forgive you for not knowing better.
I forgive you for ignoring your intuition and getting distracted.

I forgive you for not showing up fully.
I forgive you for doubting yourself.
I forgive you for talking to yourself harshly.
I forgive you for talking to others harshly.

Dear Mother,
(2019)

I'm sorry for always holding a grudge with you.
I'm sorry for getting irritated with you.
Forgive me for never feeling like I'm enough for you.
I forgive you for leaving us with our father when we were little.

I know you did the best you could.
I forgive you for speaking harshly to me and always blaming me
for your insecurities.
I forgive you for not seeing me for me.
I forgive you for introducing me to the Ishayas.
I forgive you for all the inappropriate things you've said to my
daughter.

Dear Money,
(2019)

Please forgive me for getting so frustrated with you.
You do so much for me.
You pay all my bills and allow me to do the things I want to do.

I'm sorry I treat you like you're not enough.
I know you're limitless and are always here for me.
I love you so much and I'm ready to have you in my life 100%.
I think we work really well together.

Thank you.
I love you.
Please Forgive me.

Motives
(2019)

I used to use Instagram for all my travel photos, and last night, I was looking through them all. I saw so much beauty, but what really stood out to me was all the pain. My underlying motivation for traveling.

I have a hard time posting the photos anymore because *she* doesn't feel like me. Most of my stories are along the lines of *Eat, Pray, Love*. Pilgrimages of sorts, fueled by pain, in search of transformation.

When I look back on all my trips over the past three years, there's much that's unsaid about them. I never wrote about how a broken heart is what drove me to take most of those trips, and the way I was completely transformed because of them.

How exhilarating it is to be somewhere completely unfamiliar, all alone. And at the same time, the tears you cry, alone in a hotel room.

But that's life, and that's really living! It's embracing all of it, always.

So, when I look back on all my travel photos, I see pain, and I can still feel the pain that was going on inside at the time. And I'm so damn proud of *her*. Of the woman who made it through, time and time again, when all she wanted was to give up.

And I'm inspired by the woman who stopped at nothing to make those trips happen, even when *she* was sure she would fail.

Dear Me,
(2019)

Make space for integration.

As you expand into your next level of evolution, it might take time for your outer reality to catch up with your expanded state of inner awareness.

Stay the course. All is unfolding.

Your new beliefs and realities are on their way to permeating every cell of your being.

Allow yourself to be divinely guided.

Stay open to receiving messages.

Sometimes the body has to catch up with the mind.

And sometimes the mind has to catch up with the sensations in your body.

Keep going.

Stay true to yourself.

Don't give up on your commitment to expanded states of consciousness.

You've got this!

Dear Self-Sabotage,
(2019)

I know I used to go back and forth about us breaking up, but I'm so glad we did!

I remember the good ol' days, when you used to tempt me, urging me to make choices that weren't for my highest good.

And I used to give in because I didn't think I really deserved to be happy, loved or free.

I'd be rolling along, money flowing in, feeling good, and then bam...I'd make a "stupid" financial decision that would set me back so that I could validate the story I had about myself:

"I've never been responsible with money."

I'd go through a breakup, start moving on with my life, and then you'd sneak in, whisper in my ear at 3 AM, telling me to visit an ex's Instagram profile and see how great his life looked, so that I could validate my stories of unworthiness, and feel like shit about myself.

I'd drive around with that damn AT&T router in my car for months, instead of just sending it back, and then when they charged me hundreds of dollars for it, I could validate my lifelong stories of how stupid I am, and better yet...continue to feel victimized.

Each time I thought I was done with you, you'd pop back up, and I'd feel like I was back at square one.

Oh, how I wanted you to just leave me alone, but you never respected my boundaries.

But now...now…without you, I've stepped into my power.

WITHOUT YOU, I have no doubt about the decisions I make.
WITHOUT YOU, I'm confident in who I am, and where I'm going.
WITHOUT YOU, I feel like I can breathe for the first time ever!
WITHOUT YOU, I'm done with second guessing myself.

WITHOUT YOU, I'm having the most luxurious love affair with myself!

My life now flows, with ease...and it's incredible!

I'm no longer a victim to you, Self-Sabotage.

There's no room in my life for you anymore.

I love you and appreciate all the lessons that came from our time together.

And yes, you might still come out to play every now and then, to test me.

But my energy and vibration don't allow space for your nonsense any longer!

I could tell you…
(2019 – random cell phone writing)

I could tell you about all the years of abuse…the physical, mental, sexual, spiritual and financial abuse. But that's not what this is about.

I could tell you about the eight years I spent in a spiritual cult, and the rock bottom I hit after my divorce. But again, that's not what this story is about.

I'm not going to tell you how I overcame all the trauma in my life. Although, those are some really good stories.

What I'm here to tell you about is when everything changed. When I took my power back.

I've been through therapy for years, I've had twenty years of spiritual tools at my disposal, but what it really was, was the day I woke up to my role in all of it.

Now, this isn't an easy pill to swallow. Looking back at your life and realizing it was you who actually had a very active part in all of it, even all the chaos, abuse, and trauma. But for my healing, that's what I had to do.

Here's the thing, if I want to change my life, I have to own my energy. Now, what do I mean by own my energy? It means, taking responsibility for my words and actions, and what I was willing to accept.

I fought this for a long time because I didn't want to be responsible for it. It was so much easier to play the victim. You get way more attention than when you can blame someone else. But through blaming and shaming others, all we do is give away our power to them. That doesn't hurt them, it hurts us.

And I got really tired of hurting on every level. I was exhausted…mentally, physically and spiritually. I was living in such a way that was keeping me small, dimming my light. I held back my truth to make other people feel more comfortable. I was the ultimate people-pleaser. Anything to not rock the boat.

And yeah, because of the pain I harbored inside, the boats got really, really rocky. So, I had to look at that. I had to look at what kind of energy I was putting out into the world. It came down to the simple Law of Attraction.

The energy you put out is the energy you're going to receive in return. When this hit me over the head one day it felt like a blessing and a curse, at once. I felt relieved that things weren't just happening to me all the time. I felt relieved to not feel attacked by the Universe. Or that there was something completely wrong with me.

But it also took some **radical honesty**, and that's not always easy. I had to look at my role in every single relationship that failed. I had to own my role in all the bad things I'd claimed, "just happened to me."

And so, little by little, that's what I did. I took my power back and, by taking my power back, the way I viewed the world changed dramatically. Things were no longer happening *to* me, they were just happening *around* me.

I'd been feeling as if I were constantly being attacked, and that I was only living in fear. And by living in fear, I was continuing to allow negative experiences to be drawn to me.

I remember the year I made a vow to myself that every decision I made would be based out of love, instead of fear. I wanted to see how my life would change if I were coming from this space within myself.

At first, it wasn't easy. We feel fear in our bodies and in our minds. And it can be a hard habit to break. I'd spent nearly 35 years, people-pleasing, walking on eggshells, never feeling good enough.

I didn't value myself and so, in turn, nobody else valued me, either. I didn't feel worthy, but then I was angry when other people didn't see my worth. I felt small and shy. And then wondered why I attracted certain types of people into my life who would also reinforce those feelings.

See…that's the thing with radical honesty, it can hurt you to your core. But you also know it's your truth. And the truth is always a relief, no matter how painful.

When I decided to start viewing the world in a different way, understanding how the Universe was showing up for me at the same level I was showing up for myself, and that it wasn't some grand thing that had this power over me, I was the one with the power.

In some ways, it seems so simple, and yet it's so delicately complex at the same time. It takes time to literally re-wire our brains, to ditch the old outdated habits, addictions to our pain, stress and suffering. It takes willingness, dedication and, more than anything, it takes consistency.

But I practiced until I became vigilant with my thoughts, and I started actually utilizing the tools I'd acquired over the years. And guess what happened? I started to see some progress. I would go back-and-forth between the deep healing and releasing, to the feelings of super-expanded consciousness. I was going through my own spiritual awakening.

Spiritual awakenings don't just happen once, they happen in different stages throughout your life. My first spiritual awakening was when I was eighteen. I was introduced to a higher state of consciousness, the ideas of the oneness with the Universe, and yet, I wasn't able to embody those experiences.

So, coming back to another series of spiritual awakenings nearly twenty years later left me feeling frustrated about why I hadn't gotten it before. What I had to understand and learn, however, was that every experience we go through is to get us to wake up. Even all the "bad" things that have happened, have shaped who I am today.

Once I owned my past, once I forgave myself, and forgave others, I finally owned my stories. Because it's my stories that can inspire others. It's my journeys that help others along the way.

So, then I made a conscious decision to change my energy, to change my thoughts and to really stick with it. By doing so, I watched everything change. Where I once wanted to make my life about everyone else, I now saw it differently.

The Day I Took My Power Back
(2019)

Do you know what can be the biggest motivators?

The things our family say about us, and the shit our exes say about us!

However, I didn't always feel this way. I used to let their hurtful words infiltrate my being, allowing their negativity to determine how I felt about myself.

Their words consumed my thoughts, and my energy.

I allowed them to have more control over who I was, then I had over myself.

I somehow thought they got to determine what was best for me, what I was capable of and whether my goals were realistic or not.

Even as I evolved, I let their opinions of who I used to be in the past, hold me back from fully stepping into who I was becoming.

Their words haunted me and cut me down…and I couldn't escape them.

I was exhausted – mentally, emotionally, and physically – from carrying the weight of other people's opinions.

I allowed myself to be fucked over. It's all I'd ever known. There was comfort in pain.

Until there wasn't. Until the day it all changed.

I was standing on a street, in the most romantic city in Europe, trying desperately to prove my worth and value…to someone who was adamant about not valuing or seeing me. It was hurtful, and dramatic, a scene straight out of a movie.

As I was talking, I felt myself leave my body, and I hovered above these two people, watching them, and I said to myself, "What are you doing?"

I was shocked at what I was witnessing myself do, and I made a vow at that moment:

Never again will I ever try and convince anyone that my presence is valuable, that I'm worthy of having everything in the world I desire and that I deserve an epic love. Never will I dim my light because I shine too bright for someone else's darkness.

Upon having this epiphany, I floated back down into my body, tears streaming down my face, and I said, "Thank you for everything, I love you." And…I walked away.

Everything changed that day. Everything.

Exes and family know us in ways others don't, and they also know how to hurt us in ways others don't.

But I took back my power. I became the person I'd been waiting for. I quieted the voices of my past and told them I didn't need them anymore.

I chose me. I vowed to always choose me, even when it looks or feels selfish.

I decided I was worthy, valuable and deserving, and thus, I was all of that and more.

In that moment, I stepped into the version of myself who doesn't take shit from anyone and doesn't listen to outside opinions. I used my past as fuel to set my soul on fire! To propel me forward, into the most amazing, abundant, beautiful version of myself I'd ever been!

My First Hike Without Him
(early 2019)

I drove about two hours south yesterday to go hiking at Hemlock Cliffs in the Hoosier National Forest.

There was quite a bit of foot traffic, as the weather was perfect, so after I took in the beauty of the two waterfalls, I wandered along the creek and found a secluded spot to sit and meditate.

As I did, I was flooded with unexpected emotion, so I took off my socks and shoes and stood in the water, letting this wave of tears fall and offering them back to Mother Earth. She graciously accepted them, and whispered, "It's okay to let go."

I didn't realize my first hike of the year would bring up so many memories of all my hiking last year with someone else, and the gut-wrenching type of grief that only comes from loving another so wholly and completely, and then losing them.

And as you may know, grief is the type of friend that always arrives when you least expect them, and sometimes, in your most joyful moments.

I sat with this emotion, honored it and surrendered it back to the Divine, knowing I have a lifetime of hiking memories to create ahead of me, and more love in my heart than I've ever known.

Sometimes, the concept of letting go feels like a betrayal to the other person, but really the only person we betray by holding on so tight is ourselves.

Soak in and feel the magic of this Spotify Playlist I created for Healing My Heart:

https://open.spotify.com/user/1265771279/playlist/038qaUnCT4 gZHJZKyCdTYG?si=835vOiXvQMCsMTMY1eLSlg

Chapter 5

Wild
&
Free

I find comfort in the open road and breeze through airports with a smile in my heart.

I love packing and unpacking, remembering my younger days of detachment from material possessions.

I get excited to explore the depths of my mind and consciousness and then release everything I think I know.

I feel free when I move my body. I feel wild when I howl at the moon. I chase sunsets around the world.

I'm a mermaid water baby. Drawn to the oceans, lakes, streams, hot tubs and hot springs.

I've shared lifetimes with fairies, witches and royalty.

I feel at home in the mountains, and they often call to me.

The deserts are intriguing and spark my curiosity.

I love other countries and cultures. I love being lost in a foreign city without understanding a word being spoken around me.

I love planning as much as I love spontaneity.

Solo travel thrills and excites me, and travels with friends nourish my soul.

I'm a mystery at sunrise, and I have the infectious laughter of a child.

I'm wild, free and wise beyond my years.

Even my tears are beautiful.

I'm fiery and fierce. Bold and brave. Soft and sweet.

My feet are grounded in Mama Earth.

The sun is on my face. Birds are chirping in my ear.

My adventures of awakening are getting better year by year.

Is the high worth the pain?
(2015 Atlanta)

At what point do you give into your desires? This seems to be the ultimate question.

When your body, soul and spirit want something so deeply, but your mind tells you no.

When you know the high will be the sweetest, most profound space, but you also know it can't last, and the low will feel very low.

When you have a rare connection with someone on every level and all you can think about is wanting more, more, and more.

I believe in living life to the fullest.

Whether you do or don't, there's always heartache.

And even though my mind and heart tell me no, I can't help but want what I crave, without worry.

The mind says to be more responsible, but everything else says to give into the possibilities.

So, do you pass up the opportunity of something amazing just because it can only be temporary?

I don't like her
(2015)

I don't like her
She's the one who questions everything
Who wonders

The one that won't let things go
Imagination runs wild
While emotions build

No, I don't like her
She frightens me
And gets me frazzled

She lets herself get too involved
One day she'll wake up and won't recognize herself

That's not okay
I wish she wouldn't
She needs to see what she's doing

Why can't I stop her?
She's on the loose

I want to quiet those voices in her head
The nagging that takes away her peace
I need to save her
Be her protector

She thought she had it under control
But these things get lost within her web of trust

She's afraid and confused
I think you would be too

I'll reach out my hand
In the hopes, she'll grab hold
Tell her it's safe to come in from the cold

Warm her heart by the fire
Unleash her desire
I just want to help

But she likes it better out there
Alone in the dark
It's easier that way
To protect her fragile heart

No, I don't like her
That part of me
The one who opens up so easily

In Flight
(2015)

The lonely path
Is sometimes the only path
You build your strength
From inside
But on those hard days you cry

From behind closed doors
Empty house
Empty heart
Scraping up the pieces
Of a love torn apart

These hallowed walls
Safely tucked away
In my little corner
Is where I plan to stay

Focus
Dominate
Always on top

Smile
Help
Give of yourself
More than you've got

That's why at the end of the day
I need release
Give of myself to you
Let the feelings of peace
Wash over me

Take me under your wing
Say it will be alright
You can't be going backward
If you're always in flight

Mystical Moments
(2016)

When I was eighteen, I moved to Waynesville, North Carolina, where I worked as an apprentice within a secluded meditation community. We were nestled between the Great Smokey Mountains and the famous Blue Ridge Parkway, in a way that seemed to hide us from view.

There were about a dozen houses and buildings, meditation teachers known as Ishaya Monks and us aspiring teachers.

Each day I'd walk a couple miles down the hill to a bubbling brook at the end, surrounded by fields of cows. The cows were extra-special. We had a special connection, and we would sit and talk.

Above the property there was a magical forest with a stream where I'd often see what I called fairies. They were little balls of white light bouncing around by the water. Only a couple times did they let me see their fairy-like form. At night, they'd light up the forest, and I felt at home with them.

(Side Note: Twenty years later, during a past-life regression, I would find out the fairies have always been with me, in all my lifetimes.)

Sometimes I'd be working, and I'd feel this pull to the woods, so I'd often go up there alone to see what messages I needed to hear that day.

I was seeing a man at the time, who was forty years my senior. He had a connection to the spirit world I'd never seen, and haven't since. He'd go into trance-like states, we'd listen to Enigma and he'd show me things I'd only ever experienced when taking psychedelics. He challenged every belief I'd had until then about the physical and fairy/spirit realm.

One day he took me to Asheville to visit a psychic friend of his. She spoke to me of another man who would come into my life soon and change everything. She described him in detail, and I was intrigued, but taken aback.

I started having visions of this person with so much detail, I felt I already knew him. Then one day I was standing in the office, looking out of the large picture window, when I saw somebody walking up the road to the retreat center. I felt, without a doubt, this was the person I was supposed to meet. We did meet, and before long, were madly in love.

My older man understood, but it tore him apart. At night I would hear him up in the fairy woods, running through the forest screaming my Sanskrit name. He locked himself inside one of the yurts and stayed there for days, chanting, covering his body in blood, mud and paint, as though he was a warrior fighting between man and beast.

There are days I think back to that time in my life and wonder if it was all a dream. Someday I'd like to pilgrimage back to that special, intriguing, bizarre place.

The land was sold long ago, and I wonder if the fairies stayed or if they moved on as well. Either way, they've always lived in my heart, and if I get quiet enough and conjure up just the right amount of magic, they appear.

Transformational Travel
(2018)

Travel is filled with the possibility of transformation. A lot of my biggest growth moments and massive shifts have happened while I'm traveling, and even more in the weeks returning from a big trip.

There's something to be said about having to trust that you have the ability to book a flight, get to where you're going and arrive right on time! Just getting to your destination is half the adventure.

And any adventure is as much about the inner journey as it is the outer one.

Getting out of our comfort zones opens our minds and hearts to new ideas and possibilities.

Disconnecting from the craziness of everyday life helps us reconnect with ourselves.

Travel allows us to see everything and everyone through new eyes and new perspectives.

And these new perspectives empower us to take purposeful action as we create the life we want.

This is why I travel.

Emotional Travel Baggage
(2018)

That phrase...emotional baggage...

To be honest, hearing it gives me the heebie-jeebies. It puts my stomach in knots.

I remember when I was in the dating scene, this phrase was tossed around like it was nothing, and yet nobody wanted to date someone with said emotional baggage. It was like warding off an evil creature.

Funny thing is, we all have it.

We all have experiences from our past that can still have a negative impact on us, even now.

That's what emotional baggage is. It's the backpack or suitcase full of negative, unprocessed emotions we've picked up and dragged around with us over the years. These emotions come from people, places, behaviors and experiences from our past.

So, what then is "Emotional Travel Baggage?"

It's the suitcase full of negative, unprocessed travel experiences we've had throughout our lives.

These can come from places we've visited, people we've traveled with or left behind, a negative way we felt during a particular trip or about traveling in general, even if you're not what you would call a *traveler*.

Your baggage could look like a small backpack, but the heaviness of it is still dragging you down.

Maybe it's carry-on size, but weighs so much, you have to roll it around with you. Or, just maybe, you've got so many residual travel emotions floating around, you had to cram them all inside a large, checked bag.

We've all had these experiences, right?

I know I can't be the only one who's ever missed a flight, gotten lost in a city, lost cell signal at an inconvenient time, or spent a trip arguing with a loved one.

Travel can be hard. It can test your patience and resolve. And even though we all made it through these various experiences, they can get trapped in our subconscious, whether we are aware of it or not.

What did I do when I realized I was dealing with emotional travel baggage?

I was planning a road trip for my boyfriend and I the other day, and during my planning process, I started thinking about some other road trips we'd been on together, and the negative parts of them. This didn't feel good, and I was starting to feel anxious about how this trip would go, and my mind was starting to spin.

Luckily, it was like something snapped, and I came to. I became aware of my thought process and where these thoughts were headed. Sure enough, they were up to no good!

So, I made a conscious choice to shift my thinking. I realized carrying around this emotional travel baggage from road trips past wasn't good for me or our relationship. I had to let that shit go! I had to be open to having a new experience. Otherwise, I'd just keep letting my past drag me down. And that's just not how I roll!

So, I did what I do best. I started planning how I would prepare for this five-hour drive, and I thought about what I could do differently this time to create a new and better experience.

I started putting together Spotify playlists in my head, made of lists of podcasts I've been wanting to listen to, and I downloaded an ebook. I thought about the variety of snacks we require to keep us from getting grumpy and decided when we would take turns driving. Suddenly, I was feeling positive!

Unpacking our emotional travel baggage isn't always this easy, but there are things I've learned to do, such as:

- I journal
- I talk to a friend, mentor or therapist
- I create a crystal grid around the theme of letting go

- I sit in meditation and imagine myself taking off the backpack or unpacking the suitcase (as I close it back up, I fill it with the pink light of my heart and love).
- I create travel vision boards to focus on how I want to feel on my next trip
- I move my body. I put on a song. (Both negative and positive emotions have a voice, letting me know how they want to move through my body.)
- I look back on my past, say thank you to my old experiences, and realize that even the negative experiences have shaped who I am as a traveler.

Everything we've gone through, brought us to this place we are. And here, right now, is exactly where we are each supposed to be.

We care. We do not carry.

My favorite days are these
(2018)

The ones where I'm at ease.
Where the wind blows through my hair and I'm living life
without a care.
The sun shining
Blue skies and perfect clouds

Running, resting, tuning in
Honed-in on that little voice within
Each moment new
Living for now
Productive, intentional
It all just works somehow
Don't take me away to somewhere new
All I want is to be here with you

Wanderlust
(2019)

I've always had wanderlust coursing through my veins.

A desire for adventure, and a yearning to discover every corner and crevice...of myself, and the world.

I make no apologies for my wild heart and gypsy soul.

I left normal and regular at the door, to explore the outskirts of the magical and extraordinary.

I'm not lost...I'm wandering and wondering.

I love movement and feeling the rhythmic pulse of nature.

I hold a knowing of what true freedom is.

A free spirit, with a zest for life.

Passionate and inspired by ideas, experiences and spontaneous journeys.

Contagious and magnetic energy, by simply being me.

You're drawn to me, because I am you, and you are me. And together, we can explore every realm of possibility.

We can tap into the infinite, not bound by time or space.

Would you like to join me as we venture to this place?

Freedom
(2019)

Being free isn't about rainbows and butterflies all the time.

Freedom is ebb and flow. Waxing and waning.

Allowing yourself to feel *all* the things.

Honoring when you need to dance with your shadow.

Acknowledging when things come up for you to look at.

Feeling grateful for the growth.

Freedom is listening to your body, in each moment.

It's being so tuned-in, you naturally flow with the rhythms and intuitively know what you need.

Being free means following your heart, wherever it may guide you.

It's having the power to choose.

It's the willingness and courage to come back out of the shadow, knowing you don't have to stay there for very long.

Freedom is ever-expanding. It's vast.

It's taking up all the space your heart desires.

Freedom is you.

It's who you are. Who you are meant to be.

Wild Energy
(2019)

I've always had this wild energy swirling around inside of me that, for years, I didn't know what to do with. I always knew I was a special unicorn, but I wasn't sure what my gifts actually were.

And I didn't know how to harness that energy, so I kinda just spun in circles, jumping from thing to thing, waiting for something to land.

People-pleasing was finally growing old, and I was getting sick of not knowing who I was, what I wanted, or where my place was in the world.

I'd spent over twenty years doing my spiritual "work," obsessed with self-development, and yet I would only get glimpses of my divinity. There was still a disconnect going on, and I longed to embody peak experiences.

I knew I was ready to create a life where I could make the rules, instead of following someone else's lead, but I had no idea where to start.

I'd always been a traveler, with an ache for adventure, new experiences, and seeing the world, that was getting stronger by the day.

I was more in touch with my masculine side...the hustler in me, constantly "doing" and trying to figure it all out.

My divine feminine was squelched, and I wasn't allowing myself to just be, or enjoy the simple pleasures in life, constantly striving to be someone and somewhere else.

That was, until I got bored, and everything annoyed me. Because essentially, I was annoyed with myself and who I was and wasn't being.

I'd always waged this inner war, until finally, one day, I stopped fighting and gave in.

I started shifting my energy to being the person I wanted to be, instead of wondering when she was going to show up.

And the more I practiced being her, the more I became her.

I embodied that wild child. I harnessed that swirling energy that was always there and started using it for the greater good.

Leap of Faith
(2019)

Have you ever made a decision that felt so right in your heart, but also scared the hell out of you? That's my life story!

Literally, my life has been a series of choices I've made, that haven't always been easy but have proven time and time again to be worth it.

Choices that have been downright terrifying and exhilarating, all tied into one.

Decisions that have been in complete alignment, and heart-centered, and yet I came up against resistance.

Because here's the thing...

When you're ready...like *really* ready...you'll take the leap.

And as you start to fall, it'll feel as if your arms are flailing in the air. Your hands will reach out, grasping for anything they can that feels safe and comfortable.

But there's nothing left to grasp! The safe and comfortable is no longer who you are. The you who took that leap is already someone completely different.

Because the moment you made that decision, the ground shifted beneath you. And as you're falling, you'll realize this:

The only thing you can do is surrender to this present moment in time.

As you surrender, you stop falling, and you realize you never were falling.

You were just learning how to fly!

You reach back and remember, you had wings all along.

So, you spread your wings, and start to sail through life instead of feeling like you're always going to fall and land on your ass.

That's not you anymore, because you made that really big decision, the one that altered the course of your life.

And in that moment, you're FREE!

My Iceland Memoirs

In the middle of nowhere, I learned to trust myself.

I discovered just how capable I'd become. I realized that if I'd come this far and not only survived but thrived, there wasn't anything I couldn't do.

I learned that the only one standing in my way was me. That I was the one who'd broken my heart. And I refused to be broken anymore.

I decided I wasn't going to dumb down my greatness. That I no longer could play small because I'm meant for so much more, something so much bigger than I've yet to comprehend.

I learned that pain is only temporary. That emotions come and go like the ebb and flow of life. And that they flow easier when I stop giving them so much damn power.

I discovered my voice again. In the silence of that car, in the aloneness of that vast, beautiful country, my inner goddess cried out. She begged to be heard. She quietly surfaced and rose from the ash.

I learned that everything would always be okay. Whatever trials and tribulations this life may bring, I would no longer suffer the way I had been for so long.

I grew tired. I was exhausted from fighting. *I was done.*

Done being at war with myself…and done with being at war with others.

I didn't know if I would find my peace out there. I prayed I would, but I wasn't convinced it would happen. What I found, though, was so much more than strength, peace, love or abundance.

What I found was myself.

Note: You can check out all the details on my Iceland trip in Appendix A.

Chasing the High
(2019)

I got into the world of self-development and drugs around the same time...when I was fourteen, after a suicide attempt.

I decided that if I couldn't physically leave this world, I would at least do what I could to leave my body and explore what else was going on out there in the cosmos.

For years, I excelled at exploring other realms and the depths of consciousness, however, the lows that would occur after the highs grew increasingly more painful.

There were never enough drugs. There was never enough meditation time (even at eighteen hours a day). I found euphoria through sex and even rope bondage (yes, consensual pain can actually be a very spiritual experience).

I did anything to chase the high...exercise, sex work, hiking way past my physical limits.

These things aren't all negative, and there's nothing wrong with wanting the experience of oneness, bliss and unity. That's the truth of who you are. But those things aren't feelings or emotions. They're states of being.

And what I've learned to cultivate over the past 25 years on my adventure of awakening is how to maintain a state of bliss no matter what's going on externally.

I see a whole lot of self-development out there and not enough conscious conversations, so that's what I'm here to bring!

Zion
(July 2019)

If there was ever a perfect day, it was this one in July 2018. Zion National Park in Springdale, Utah is nothing short of magical, and hiking to Observation Point was challenging in every way for me but completely worth it!

It blows my mind this was just one year ago, and how everything in my life has changed since then.

Everything!

I didn't plan on any of this a year ago. The things I'm doing now weren't even on my radar...consciously. And I'd no clue what would transpire after this trip.

It's funny because getting to Zion wasn't easy.

When we arrived at the airport, our flight had been canceled, and we weren't able to rebook until the next evening, which meant missing the whole weekend.

My partner at the time had booked this trip for my birthday, and I was dead set on going. However, our options were to cancel the whole thing, or fly another airline for three times the price, which my partner wasn't willing to cover.

So, I had to make a quick decision!

Would I cave into the fear of not having the money come back as easily as it went out, or would I go on this epic trip to Zion National Park?

I bought the ticket, never looked back, and I'm still alive today!

That trip took trust. It took patience. It took perseverance and pushing my limits, on all levels. And for me, that's the most exhilarating experience I can have!

Even when we have "perfect" plans, we're still living in the unknown. Nothing is ever set in stone, so we can choose to flow with the river, or resist it. But ultimately, it's our choice!

I choose to take the risks, do what scares me and get uncomfortable! That's where the true enjoyment of life actually exists. Otherwise, I miss out on all the magic.

OWN IT
(2019)

OWN the fact that you're different.
OWN that you're meant to stand out.
OWN that you have magic coursing through your veins.
OWN that you feel things deeply.
OWN your wild.
OWN your wisdom.
OWN that you're tuned into a higher frequency.
OWN that you're craving freedom NOW.
OWN that you require conversations with depth.
OWN that you're the only one holding you back.
OWN the fact that you sense things others don't.
OWN your sensitivity.
OWN that you need time in nature to recharge.
OWN that you follow the cycles of the moon.
OWN that the stars and planets are your guides.
OWN your free spiritedness.
OWN the fact that you are a sacred being.
OWN that you know you're meant for more.
OWN that you're READY.

Dance in your living room, naked.
Run wild through the forest.
Chase sunsets until your heart's content.
Pray, even when someone's watching.
Laugh loud.
Take up space.
Breathe deep.
Let bliss fill your soul.
Connect.

Take that step.
Make that leap.

Climb that mountain.

And don't look back.

Hey, Wild Child!
(2019)

I know you have this energy swirling around inside of you.
You want to create MAGIC.
You want to create FREEDOM.
You want to create ABUNDANCE from doing what you love!
To live a life where YOU make the rules.
A life where you feel lit up AF!
Where things flow to you effortlessly because your energy is so magnetic!
You know you didn't come here to live a mediocre life.
But you're holding back.
You're not sure if it's safe to step out so boldly.
You dip your toe in, and then back out because you aren't quite confident enough in your abilities...YET.
You still have old stories running in the background that are disconnecting you from Spirit.
From remembering that there is infinite energy at your disposal, when you're open to receiving.
You think you have to have it all figured out, and because you don't, you don't take action.
You ARE ready to release control, but it feels like a free fall.
And you aren't sure who's going to be there when you land.
What if I told you there is no landing?
You can free fall, spread your wings and FLY!
You can harness that wild energy into a source of all CREATION.
It's okay to be afraid. But you don't have to be paralyzed!
Don't just talk about living Wild and Free...EMBODY it!

These are MY people!
(Sedona 2019)

The ones who are up for adventure.
The ones in flow.
The ones with wild and free spirits.
The ones who will dance on mountaintops, and howl at the moon with me.
The ones hungry for transformation, and are willing to do what it takes to get there.
The ones with big hearts, and so much light to shine upon the world.
The ones not just talking about doing it, but are actually walking the talk!
The ones who value presence, and experience magic in a tangible way.
The ones who show up, and are ready, now.
These are the beautiful goddesses on this incredible journey with me.
Sacred Sisterhood. Sacred Connections. Sacred Bonds.
This is the Sacred Connection Retreat.

Only you have the power to transform your life, but together we can change the world, and raise the collective consciousness!

Moldable
(2019)

I used to be moldable.

I was so lost and confused, that I tried on a million hats, trying to find the one that fits.

I was desperate to be liked. Desperate to be loved. And desperate to "fit in."

Funny thing is I always knew I would never "fit in" because that's not me.

But I didn't think who I was, would ever be enough.

So, I'd mold into who I thought everyone else wanted me to be.

I thought if I blended in, I'd never feel the pain of standing out.

Funny thing is, I always stood out.

It wasn't until I started traveling alone, that I really discovered who *Kelsey* was.

What her likes and dislikes were. What makes her tick. What lights her the fuck up!

And then I started dancing again.

But not the salsa dancing I used to do, which was all for show and getting techniques perfect. Forget that.

I learned how to start moving my body in ways that felt good for *me*.

And now when I dance, I hardly even recognize myself. There are a flow and ease of being so completely present in my body.

I'm unashamed of being a sensual, feminine creature whose movements are sometimes small, and other times take up as much space as the room can hold.

It was through getting out of my head, and into my body, that I honed my intuition. I started becoming so aware of the subtleties in my energy and emotions, and what they mean.

And I started to really listen.

I began to trust myself. And through trusting myself, I took off all the hats. I stopped letting them define me.

● ● ●

I'm not a wife/girlfriend/lover. I'm not even just a mother.

I'm not who you want or expect me to be.

I'm me, wholly and completely me.

Goddess, Priestess, Queen.

And this goddess dresses in ways that light *me* up. I speak in ways that are authentic to *my* being. I only go places that feel good to *me*. I interact with people who are in alignment with who I am.

Do not let the world define you.

You are more than a wife or lover. You are more than someone's mom.

You are here to stand out, make ripples and be different.

Free Spirits don't fit in. We don't want to fit in.

We crave freedom.

We were born with a calling in our souls.

We are here to be the change-makers, the shifters, the Light Workers. We are here to make a massive fucking impact on the world.

Let's do this!

Soak in and feel the magic of this Spotify Playlist I created for Wild & Free:

https://open.spotify.com/user/1265771279/playlist/6jNIQ9wcNT
9EjA1ouaJHOo?si=fqLXEGdOSTWLr25e6TeQEA

Iceland, February 2017

Iceland, February 2017

New Mexico, July 2017

Taos, New Mexico, July 2017

Boulder, Colorado, August 2017

Garden of the Gods, Colorado, August 2017

Garden of the Gods, Colorado, August 2017

Arkansas Crystal Mining, November 2017

Bruge, Belgium, May 2018

Czech Republic, January 2019

Prague, Czech Republic, January 2019

Sedona, Arizona, April 2019

Austin, Texas, September 2019

Austin, Texas, September 2019

Chapter 6
Crystal Clear

I process my pain through poetry and become the ultimate shadow dancer. Then I talk it out. The prose flows, and I become crystal clear.

In or Out
(2016)

I could pull back
Let my fear take the wheel
Always wonder what might have happened
What we could have been

I could lose my mind living in the future
Worried about how easily he could break me
Continue with my anxiety
Living my life in apprehension
Keeping my walls up and my heart guarded

Or...

I could let go and be present
Appreciate the happy times
Let my feelings of anxiety turn into butterflies
Layout the broken pieces of my heart for him to see
Allow us to just "be"

It's a moment to moment choice
And it's a battle of heart and mind
But if I don't open my eyes to what's there
I will forever live blind

I trust
(2017)

My Intuition
My Path
My Tribe
In the Journey
All will be well
I will be supported
How it feels
My daughter is cared for

Lessons from Mercury Retrograde
(2018)

Today marks the last day of the Mercury Retrograde, and I'm feeling a sense of relief.
Mercury went retrograde on November 17th, and OMG, have I been feeling it big-time.

Note: Whether you're familiar with this planetary alignment or not, here's a little Mercury Retrograde refresher...
Three to four times a year, Mercury's orbit slows down, creating the illusion that it's moving in reverse. And during this time, all things associated with Mercury go freakin' haywire.
It's recommended not to make any big decisions or major purchases during a time of Mercury Retrograde, and be prepared for miscommunications, delayed travel, and watch for electronics acting up.

I personally experienced major disruptions in communication within my relationships the past couple weeks, my phone and computer have been randomly shutting down, and even my car decided not to start one morning!
Let's throw my boyfriend's birthday, a trip to Colorado, Thanksgiving and my daughter's birthday in the mix, too, just for added fun!
Here's the good news, though...the Mercury Retrograde season can be frustrating, but it's not all bad, and I've gained much wisdom during this time as well.
The Retrograde allows us to reassess, revisit, readdress, redo and redesign our lives. It also allows us to stop, pause and listen.
We can all benefit from slowing down and taking a closer look at situations with greater depth, which happens when Mercury retrogrades.
Here's what's been going on with me the past few weeks:

I've been presented with opportunities to revisit past family trauma and hurt, and I can now say I've healed from it.

The Universe has asked me to reassess my money mindset and shift to the energy of limitless abundance, asking me to step up. And you better believe, I am!

I'm readdressing old ways of interacting and communicating with people, and how they no longer serve. Then taking conscious action to switch to healthier communication skills.

I'm redesigning my business in a way that feels super-expansive and in the flow.

I'm learning to not react. Instead, I'm taking a moment to pause and then act from there.

This has been a time of deep reflection and dancing with my shadow. There's been deep grief, pain and sorrow, accompanied by lots of tears.

But it's also been a time of relearning to use my voice and a time of deep empowerment. And this has made it all worth it.

Today, Mercury goes direct, but that doesn't mean we are in the clear! I personally am already feeling the veil being lifted, however, it's recommended to allow at least two days, minimum, after Mercury moves ahead to normal direct speed, before starting projects, making those big purchases or decisions.

We don't have to let the planets rule us, but we can make more sense of our experiences by understanding how their alignments do in fact affect us.

Fixing
(2019)

When he tells you he's an asshole, don't be surprised when his actions mirror those of an asshole.

When he says he'll destroy you if he stays, it's not an invitation to prove him otherwise.

If he's addicted to porn, that's not going to magically change because you're now in the picture.

If he doesn't know what he wants, it's not cute and should not be taken on as a project.

Your "helping" isn't helping anyone. If someone isn't clear about how they feel about you, there's really nothing you can do to create that clarity for them.

We can inspire others, but we can't make them be somewhere they aren't in their lives or personal growth.

You can't force someone to change. People change on their own accord.

You either accept them for who they are and the relationship for what it is, or you decide you want more than what they're offering.

But staying in a relationship where one person isn't willing or able to be more will only stunt your growth.

There's also nothing wrong with these men! Just because they aren't where you want them to be doesn't mean they deserve to be shit on either.

Men generally show us, and a lot of the times even tell us, who they are, if we're listening. It's us women who seem to hear something different or don't listen at all. We take what they say as a challenge, to fix, help or change them into the best possible versions of themselves they can be.

Well, guess what? That's not our job! We're not their therapist or life coach.

There's nothing wrong with me if they choose not to grow. There's nothing wrong with me if they choose to leave. There's nothing wrong with me if they won't change their behaviors or mindset. There's nothing wrong with me!

But staying places where I'm not celebrated, appreciated and cherished will leave me feeling like everything's wrong.

My unwavering love isn't always the magic elixir.

My endless devotion isn't always what they need.

My light will sometimes cast shadows.

But I will not dim or dumb down who I am to appease them.

My Year Without Men
(2019)

Why did I decide to take a year off from dating? Because I never have before.

Boys arrived in my life at a very young age, and I quickly became addicted to them.

I was addicted to the attention I received, the way I suddenly felt that I had value and even the way they hurt me.

As a child, I was extremely shy. Like so shy it's painful to think about. So, when I was fourteen and had a 21-year-old suddenly take an interest in me, I was thrust into a whole new world of sex, drugs and lies.

Bogged down with insecurities, it was the perfect recipe for codependency, also known as relationship addiction. It's an excessive emotional or psychological reliance on a partner and is rapidly becoming more common.

The way this played out for me was by being in one relationship after another. And if I wasn't in an actual relationship, I always had people on the side to call for attention, affection or sex.

There's a saying: "The best way to get over someone is to get under someone else." Well, let's just say I had made that my life's mantra.

So, every time a relationship would end, I'd be completely devastated. And instead of sitting with my pain, and giving myself space to heal, I'd fill that space with anything or anyone, to essentially numb out and forget, rather than feel.

Each new relationship I entered into came with baggage that I hadn't released from the last one. I never truly gave myself the time or space I needed to heal or integrate the lessons.

Twenty-four years later, I'm in a completely different space…physically, spiritually and emotionally. My desires have changed. My relationship with my body has changed. And what I require in connection with another has dramatically changed.

July 2nd marks 7 months since the abrupt ending of my most recent relationship. This was one of the most significant relationships of my life, in a lot of ways, and it's still taking time to release from my psyche and body.

And as my birthday is 7/7, and 7s have always been significant for me, this 7-month anniversary of ending that relationship, in the 7th month of the year, feels very significant.

The way I've approached this breakup has been different than ever before. As gut-wrenching as it's been, I've chosen to take every lesson I can from it and consciously grow from the experience.

Part of the healing process has been forgiveness of self. It's been owning up to my role in all my relationships, honoring who I was at each moment in time, and forgiving myself for not knowing, or being better. Owning my part is essential to the forgiveness process, as difficult as it can be. There are always two people involved.

Another part of my process has been seeing how much of my worth and value I placed in the hands of another. Seeing how devastating it's been when I haven't felt valued by someone else, and when I've felt I had to prove myself to them. That's been hard to digest for sure.

And finally, seeing how much of my worth has been based around my body, and what I have to offer someone sexually. And I'm choosing to end that cycle of abuse from others, and most importantly, self-abuse.

I'm taking this year off from men, to sit in silence with myself. Who knows, it might even go longer...

I now know the person I want to be, and where I want to be in my life, for the next time I enter into a relationship. And I'm not quite there yet, and that's okay!

I'm spending more time alone than ever before, and in turn...I'm falling in love...with me. And not just falling in love with myself, but actually liking myself, too. That's a biggie.

I'm seeing how fun I am, how silly I am, how sensual, giving and loving I am. I'm truly seeing what it is I have to bring to the table, and I'm no longer willing to compromise on what I require in a partnership.

I'm truly learning who I am without another. I'm tapping into my intuition more than ever before, because I've drowned out the noise and outside energies. Not only am I spending most of my time alone, but in a lot of silence.

I am discovering my voice, and who I am. I'm finding out what I really like and don't like. I'm seeing what values are most important to me, and I'm committed to myself in all ways.

I don't numb out the pain, or the heartache or the yearning. I choose to take them all as my dance partners. And when our dances are done, the light returns, shining brighter than ever before.

People keep asking me if the strong urges for sex or a relationship arise. And to be honest, not that much. And that's totally different for me! It's completely unfamiliar territory.

Of course, holidays and weekends are the hardest (or when I'm ovulating!), when it's natural to crave affection, but I move through it and sit in gratitude for what I do have in my life…which is a crazy amazing support system.

I've mastered orgasmic manifestation. (It's a thing…look it up!) I get to choose what turns me on and makes me tick. I get to dress up in the middle of the day, at home alone…just because it makes me feel good.

I've developed this beautiful outlook on how I view my body as this sacred temple. And I have no desire to give it over to someone who doesn't also respect and view me as such.

I'm spending time in conscious women's groups, so I can learn from my past and find out how to make different choices in future relationships.

I know a lot of people go this length of time without someone in their life, but for me, this is massive. This is me stepping into a healthier version of myself, living the way she would act and treat herself.

This has nothing to do with bashing the masculine. It's quite the opposite. By staying away from men, I'm actually learning more about them than ever before, and I'm understanding why they are the way they are. I'm seeing that there are conscious men out there!

I have no idea what this next five months have in store for me in the relationship department, and I'm good with that. For now, I'm focused on me, my healing and building my business.

The one-year mark in December will also be my daughter's birthday, so I plan on celebrating my rebirthing, too!

Being alone isn't something our culture embraces, and yet, when it's done with purpose and intention, it can be the most magical, enlightening and awakening journey of your life!

I'm not waiting for someone else to make me happy. I am happy now, and that someone else will show up when I'm whole, complete and fulfilled within myself. I thought I was at that place before, but now I see I still have a long way to go. Now, I'm getting it, though. And I just keep loving myself...always!

Tired of Being Tired
(2019)

Exhaustion used to plague me.
I'd wake up every morning dreading the day.
I wasn't just physically tired.
My soul felt I'd already lived a hundred lives in one lifetime.
I was tired of struggling.
Tired of not living up to my potential.
Tired of feeling stuck.
Tired of feeling powerless.
Tired of being a victim to my circumstances.
Tired of not LIVING.
Tired of feeling like I wasn't capable of turning my dreams into reality when I knew inside I was destined for greatness.
Just so damn tired, no matter what I did.
Until the day it all changed, just like that.
I went on a pilgrimage that awakened my soul.
I woke up to a remembering.
I took my power back.
I discovered how capable I am.
I remembered WHO I AM.
The calling was heard.
And I followed the call while continuing to ask, "What's next?"
So, the next phase of my journey began.
My travels lit a spark until a flame began burning.
And now a FIRE is spreading!
I'm on a mission to make my life the most magical experience ever.
I'm here to help light that spark in myself and others, so that we can do the epic shit we came to this planet to do.
I wake up each day ready for whatever life throws my way.
The edge of leaping into the unknown, yeah, it still feels scary.
But epic shifts happen the moment you decide and commit.
That's what has happened to me.

I was tired of being tired.

I am committed to...
(2019)

I am committed to staying true to myself.

I am committed to going forward, not backward.

I am committed to growth and expansion.

I am committed to being the highest expression of my authentic self.

I am committed to falling in love with myself.

I am committed to doing what feels right.

I am committed to never giving up or giving in.

I am committed to owning my truth and power.

I am committed to being of service in the highest possible way.

I am committed to feeling amazing in my feminine body.

I am committed to ever-expanding joy and light.

I am committed to being the woman my daughter needs me to be.

I am committed to being an example.

I am committed to paving the way.

Do you even like yourself?
(2019)

It's one thing to be all about self-love, and do all the things to love on myself, which most people refer to as self-care. And I'm a big fan!

However, it's another thing altogether to actually *like* myself.

It's the same way we can have love in our hearts for someone else, but not actually like their words or actions. So, do I like myself? Do I even know how to learn to like myself?

For starters, I pay attention to how I talk to myself. Am I constantly focusing on what I don't like, or am I celebrating my strengths and gifts?

On my journey to discovering how much I like myself, this meant spending a lot of time alone.

I spent time traveling alone, so I could really hone-in on my wants and needs. When we travel by ourselves, we get to see what we want to do at every moment, without any outside opinions. It's called intuition...and it becomes our saving grace.

The first time I experienced this was heaven on earth! I couldn't believe how much time I'd spent catering to other people, or going with the flow of what others wanted, rather than doing what I actually wanted to do.

And then it took spending lots of time alone, at home.

Was I able to sit in silence with myself, or even be by myself, for any length of time?

For most people, that's a big NO!

Some of us are more social creatures than others. However, if you're constantly needing to surround yourself with others to feel comfortable, my guess is you're not really comfortable with yourself, and who you are.

Aloneness isn't easy for most people, but it's the place you get to tap into for deeper levels of self-awareness. It's where you get to see the parts of yourself you might not like so much...or you realize how much you do like yourself!

For me, it's been a realization of how awesome I am, even with all my quirks.

So, on the journey towards self-love & self-care, I'm not forgetting to like myself as well!

All the weird, quirky, magical and fabulous parts of me!

And what I'm experiencing is my confidence skyrocketing in all areas of my life, and I've stopped settling for things that don't feel good for me.

And finally, I realize that I'll never believe anyone likes me as much as they do, if I don't like me, too.

How are you showing up in relationships?
(2019)

I used to complain about my romantic partners "not showing up" for me. And I hear this complaint from others about their partners, all the time!

They weren't being who I wanted them to be, and I blamed and projected my shit onto them, instead of owning my part in it.

My part is to look at how I'm showing up!

If I'm being triggered, it's because there's something going on inside of me.

Everyone around us is a mirror, and our romantic relationships, especially, mirror back to us all our wounded parts, parts we don't always want to look at and do the work to heal.

Even if I have a partner who loves me and wants to be there for me, if I don't love myself, and am not willing to do the work it takes to get there, I'll never truly feel the love from someone else. They'll always be inadequate because I feel inadequate.

If I want a partner who's confident and "emotionally available," is my energy radiating confidence, and am I emotionally available?

We attract the energy into our lives that we put out into the world, consciously and unconsciously.

Wouldn't it feel a hell of a lot better if I could own my energy and learn how to call in what I really want and deserve, rather than letting my unconscious mind run the show?

Betrayal, Forgiveness, Power
(2019)

To forgive we must understand.
Understand that it's not personal.
Understand they acted from where they were.
Understand that it was karmic.

They didn't cheat.
They had sex.
And they had sex because they were void of something.
Longing.
Searching.

We are Always the Teacher & the Student
(2019)

We are always the Teacher and the Student.

If you ever think you're not the student, you're not living in purity, but in arrogance.

For eight years, I lived in a community of hierarchy, and it's been a long journey of unwinding those belief systems.

We had our Teachers, basically gurus, and they were apparently at some advanced level of consciousness, that was made clear to us that we would never attain.

Then there was the "elite" group. They just happened to be the gurus' favorite students, so they were labeled as being in a higher state of consciousness, but not too high. Just enough to be better than the rest of us. The ones to be in envy of.

In the end, these belief systems led to the suicide of a very close friend of mine. His striving to be perfect, and feeling like he couldn't achieve it, made him end his life.

I was always just on the outskirts. Not quite in the elite, but close enough to our teachers to see enough of the shit that went on behind the scenes.

I was never good enough. I fought against my own mind, day in and out, for years. I never understood why I couldn't just shut my mind off like I thought everyone else was.

And I certainly was never quite cool enough, either. I was so insanely insecure within myself, that I felt like a floater, not really fitting in anywhere.

Now, I see what a gift that was! Even though I, too, strived to "get" to the next level, it kinda felt icky to me, at the same time. Of course, back then, I was brainwashed into not trusting my innate wisdom, my Intuition. So, I didn't really question it too deeply.

I'm very sensitive now to anyone who puts themselves above anyone else, and that's something I never want to be in a position of, either.

Intense therapy for the past three years has helped me shed these layers of conditioning.

Every time I meet someone really awesome, I share with my therapist about them, and she's always skeptical. Not of them, but of me.

Because the way I'd talk about people was in a way that put them above me.

I was still thinking that these mentors, coaches and people I looked up to had something I didn't. This played out in my romantic partnerships as well.

And I also remember the day it all shifted...

I stopped putting others above me. I stopped thinking I had to get somewhere other than where I am. I stopped ignoring my gut instincts.

I stopped putting other people up on a pedestal!

And I started seeing myself in a whole new light!

And it's amazing!!

I get more out of my relationships because nobody is better than another.

I was able to lead an awesome retreat in Arizona, from a place of purity. From knowing I have so many amazing gifts and experiences to share with the world, and I did share them, with those women.

But I also learned so much, as we were all equals.

This shift has taken me nearly twenty years to make, and it may always be something I have to keep an eye on.

But please know, that I don't see you as anymore, or any less. We are all just going down different roads. We all have our own journeys and lessons.

The power is inside each of us.

We have people in our lives to help guide us, and that's what I'm here to do, but not to take others' power away, or make them feel as if they're never going to get to where I am or someone else is.

Any good coach, or leader, sees you in complete perfection, and is there to help you remember who you are!

You have to start BEFORE you're ready
(2019)

You'll never be your perfect version of "readiness."

That's just fear keeping you from spreading your wings and taking that flight!

So, step up, step out, do what you're being called to do.

No matter how small or how big the step is, you are ready RIGHT NOW!

Sacred Vows
(2019)

I am ready to be done with self-abuse, fear and scarcity.

I am ready to wake up to the truth of who I really am, in a deep and profound way.

I vow to:

Let go of self-sabotage.
Give up self-loathing.
Stop the self-abuse.
Be a vixen, instead of a victim.
Love every inch of myself.

These vows are potent, and powerful, and are only for those who are ready to deeply embrace their magic.

And I'm ready!

Letter from my Future Self
(2019)

Dearest Kelsey,

I promise you it's all going to work out, even better than you can imagine. It's not necessary to get wrapped up in the stories. Say thank you and *let them go*.

It's time for you to rise up. Not too long from now, you'll be traveling on the weekends, exploring and going on more adventures. But you have to *believe*!

You have to stop looking to the outside or relying on anyone else. Build your tribe, your circle. They will sustain you and keep you grounded and connected.

It feels so rewarding and incredible to be talking with so many women every day who are inspired by you and want to be around your energy, more and more.

Keep believing!

Values
(2019)

We all have different values, and priorities.

Some people's highest values include nutrition, bodybuilding, traveling the world, outdoor adventures, going out to eat or concerts.

And then there are people whose #1 priority, is vibration, energy, mindset and growth. They're driven by conscious evolution.

I'm one of those people. And those are the people I spend my energy on, and my time with.

We all have different priorities, and that's totally cool. If we were all the same, it wouldn't be as fun!

But if our values don't match up, we aren't going to match up.

I will only spend time with and work with people whose highest value is also growth and conscious evolution.

And I won't compromise on that, in any way.

Because when you're so hungry for change you can barely stand it, have had enough with just getting by, and are willing to do whatever it takes to shift into a space of inspiration and magic, then we can talk.

And if that's just not your priority, that's okay. But whatever your highest values are, own that shit!

I was born a helper and a healer...but that translated into "fixing." For a good portion of my life, I tried to fix people who weren't really wanting to do the work to help themselves. And that's exhausting!

I've since developed a greater sense of self-love and self-worth, which includes healthy boundaries, and only helping people who genuinely want to do the work and who put in the time and energy it takes to do the deep soul work. And nothing is more fulfilling!

Messy Action
(2019)

My favorite phrase the past month has been "messy action."

For me, it means taking action, even if I don't feel ready. Even if there's fear. Even if I don't have an exact plan.

Messy action is courageously stepping into the unknown, knowing that by taking that first step, I'm putting energy in motion.

I can't remember a time where I actually felt ready for anything.

I planned to leave my marriage for two years, trying to get all the logistics worked out. Until my plan never came together, and I up and left one day, with $50 to my name, no job, no car and no home. And it was the best decision I ever made!

When I decided to leave my job recently, I just knew I had to do it. Like all my other major life decisions, there wasn't a plan, a strategy or much else to it…except a dream and a vision.

Taking messy action is letting go of this false idea of perfection. It's being bold and brave.

It's standing in my power and knowing I don't have to have it all figured out. And finding a slight sense of excitement in that.

Taking messy action is allowing things to unfold. It's staying present and trusting.

I'm longing to create something more, something different!

I'm being called to step into the next phase of my journey.

And by holding myself back, getting lost in "analysis paralysis," and not following my truth…I'm doing myself a disservice, and all those around me.

There's no time like now.

The Art of BE-ing
(2019)

I've been practicing more and more The Art of BE-ing – rest and self-care, as an embodied state, rather than "things" on my to-do list.

I've created this magical space in my life, where I have the time/freedom to feel into what my body, mind and spirit need in each moment.

I'm shifting the paradigm around what "working" looks like, and how it feels. And you know what? If it doesn't feel good, I don't do it. It's that simple.

Someone asked me the other day if I do "energy work" in my coaching sessions. I thought the question was curious. So, after the conversation, I sat with it.

What I've concluded is that energy work is my way of being. No, I'm not constantly doing focused Reiki, for example. However, all day long, I'm playing with energy, and I am tuned into where my energy is.

Before I get on a coaching call, I clear my energy, so I can be a clear channel. That's my energy work. I allow spirit to move through me, in everything I do and say.

When I write, it's energy work. I'm transmitting energy through words, and onto paper, or a screen…for others to take in and absorb. And I'm conscious of the energy I'm working with so that it comes through with the highest possible value.

With this type of work, it requires me to be a state of BE-ing, instead of DO-ing, at all times.

It requires rest when I need to rest and integration.

It requires doing whatever I need to do to keep myself in alignment. And when I'm in alignment, my actions & inspiration come from that space…not from my head or my to-do list.

The Art of BE-ing – rest and receiving – takes practice for me, as it's not how I was raised. There are a lot of ingrained belief systems to bust through.

That said, with dedication, it's the most profoundly enjoyable state to embody.

How to Practice Receiving
(2019)

I used to feel guilt or shame when someone gave me something. It might've been offered to me with no strings attached, and yet, I still couldn't help but feel anxious about it.

I've spent most of my life in that space. Always the perfectionist, the people-pleaser, feeling like I had to do everything on my own, without help. Asking for help meant weakness.

But since I always put myself in a position where I had to ask for help, I would feel like the other person had one up on me, or I'd put them up on a pedestal, feeling less than they were.

It created a lonely inner world, filled with self-judgment, shame and self-loathing for never living up to my insanely high expectations of myself.

I tended to get tripped up wanting to control how abundance looked in my life, or where it was coming from. But I also knew I had to actually be open to receiving from others, and the Universe, because we aren't meant to be in this world alone! We are meant to be in collaboration and community, and we're meant to support one another in whatever ways we can.

I had an experience recently where someone gave me money, seemingly out of nowhere, with complete love, and no strings attached.

And for the first time in my life, I felt what it's like to really receive something, without guilt or shame. *Happy dance!* I thought I'd been open to receiving before, but this experience reverberated throughout my entire body.

It didn't even feel personal with this person. It literally felt like the Universe itself giving to me.

And that's exactly how it should feel any time we receive anything. Guilt and shame aren't required to be in the mix. We are worthy of receiving, simply by existing and being us.

Because when we're giving, in all ways, we're going to receive in all ways.

So, I'll say it again…I am worthy of receiving, and I don't have to do this dance of life on my own!

I'm worthy of receiving the love I want, the desires in my heart and more financial abundance than I can dream of, with the support of heart-centered connections.

There's so much more fluidity when we surrender, release control and our attachments to how we think things "should" look.

The Universe is infinite, and there's abundance all around us. The more we give, the more we receive!

Back to Wholeness
(2019)

On Wednesday mornings, I attend my friend Susan's Qoya women's circles, and this morning, I pulled card number 38 – Essence.

(Note: Each circle, we pull a Tarot card from the altar in the center of our circle.)

My card read:

"Life is a school that we move and graduate through, learning many things as we cloak ourselves in environmental knowledge. You are on the warrior's path toward enlightenment, and one day, you will peel away this accumulated knowledge like layers of an onion, moving back into the source of your power."

This card has felt more perfect and powerful throughout the day, and especially so as I was chatting with one of my mentors about my upcoming birthday, and the significance around it.

That's when I realized…it was card 38 for my 38th birthday!

Nearly 25 years on my spiritual path, and I'm overflowing with the knowledge and wisdom I've gathered throughout this lifetime.

And all that knowledge is really just moving me back to my source of power, now at an accelerated pace, so I can share my magic, medicine and message with the world.

The card continued:

"The experience of life is the process of piecing together these scrambled fragments into one great mandala that reflects back the one source of all beings."

This part reminds me of the process of spiritual awakening, and when you can look back on your life with nothing but gratitude for all of it, knowing it's all brought you to this very point in time, exactly where you are meant to be.

There are no accidents or victims. We chose our experiences before we even came into this life, and our job is to keep opening up more and more to this awakened adventure, back to wholeness.

Summer Solstice Magic
(2019)

This Summer Solstice season has me feeling the winds of change blowing in…and I'm loving and embracing every minute of it!

June has brought about lots of quiet, deep reflection, release and rest. And our weather here in Indiana has mirrored that, with endless rain and chilly temps. It's felt quite perfect in a way.

And then the solstice – the longest daylight hours of the year – brought the sunshine with it, and that's exactly how it feels in my heart.

Something big is happening and is on its way. And I don't know what it is yet, but whatever it is, it feels joyful and a breath of fresh air.

The Summer Solstice is about burning through what's no longer serving the fire that's burning inside of you, to create what you're desiring in this world.

I was blessed with leading a Qoya Summer Solstice Celebration, where we collectively opened this magical, healing portal that I'm still feeling into and embracing, which directly reflected our theme of the night – Embracing the Light.

We danced and shared with one another how it feels to embrace the light within ourselves, and others. And what it's also like to embrace the shadow aspect, and not want to, or be able to, return to the light.

We went deep into our shadows, and it was powerful to witness, as we all emerged and found our way back to the light, our true essence.

Nothing nourishes and feeds my soul more than in-person, conscious connection, and tonight, we were in sisterhood, as we embraced the totality of who we are.

Turning my Back on Spirituality
(2019)

Yesterday, I went Live on Facebook, talking about how I turned my back on my spiritual path for a long time after leaving a spiritual cult I was in for eight years.

The thing is I thought being spiritual had to look a certain way, and I was taught I essentially had to give up everything to attain enlightenment.

So, I gave up all worldly possessions, lived in seclusion from the "outside" world, dressed only in white, relinquished my name, took on a Sanskrit one and surrendered my life to a Teacher...from the ages of 18-26.

I had some pretty incredible, exalted, ascended experiences, learned techniques for heightened awareness and focused solely on consciousness, but ultimately didn't exactly find what I was searching for, as the teachings were distorted by human egos.

When I gave up that lifestyle, I left with a bad taste in my mouth for spirituality...and so I turned my back on my path.

Essentially, it was still my path. I just chose the hard way after my departure from that community, going through nearly ten years of what's called The Dark Night of the Soul.

Many years of feeling completely lost, unfocused and disconnected from the truth of who I am. I went in the complete opposite direction.

It was when the pain became so unbearable, I was tired of living and I wanted to give up that I returned to my spiritual practices. Except, this time, I did it differently. I did it in a way that felt expansive and liberating, instead of someone else telling me how enlightenment was "supposed" to look.

I discovered that the true test of awareness and consciousness comes with waking up every single day and staying committed to the path, even when existing in this physical world feels challenging.

And I've picked up new tools, other than basic meditation, that have propelled my growth further than ever before, by embracing all aspects of Self.

There's no one, right way to journey along your path of awakening. It looks different for each and every being.

The thing is once you get a taste for just how magical you are, and you experience the oneness of the Universe and the lightness of your being, anything other than that can feel really constricting.

High Vibe
(2019)

High vibe isn't a feeling or emotion.

For a while there, I was getting caught up in the idea that I had to be "high vibe" all the time. Always "on."

So, I've been diving deeper into what that means, and how it resonates in my body.

And here's what I concluded:

♥ Being "on" can be quiet and pensive.

♥ Being "on" can mean acknowledging and honoring when the shadow self presents itself, and courageously dancing with it.

♥ High vibe, for me, means making sure that the vibration of my being is in alignment with my truth.

♥ It's not an emotion.

♥ We wouldn't appreciate the longest day of the year, without going through the darkest day of the year.

♥ High vibe is shifting my mindset and being committed and dedicated to my path, no matter what I'm feeling.

Pressure
(2019)

We put so much pressure on ourselves. We stay in places, relationships, jobs, etc. because we're scared of the unknown. We're comfortable in our discomfort.

As kids, we were taught to tough it out, even if we didn't like something. And as we grew up, there was a tendency to do things because it was the "right thing" or the "next best step."

But the truth is, it's not what you really want. It just looks and sounds good on paper or fits others' expectations of being "rational."

The thing is, we outgrow relationships all the time. The job you have might not be a good fit anymore. That neighborhood you moved to isn't perhaps what it was once cracked up to be.

We make decisions on a daily basis, but where are these decisions coming from?

The truth is you want to do something else, you want to be your own boss, open your own business or you want a better job.

Maybe you want to travel more, or move into a new house, but you feel stuck taking care of kids and paying bills.

We put our lives on hold and we stay somewhere, usually our comfort zone, because we don't want to rock the boat.

We so desperately want to do the right thing, and in doing so, we keep giving away our power.

And here's the thing…It didn't feel good to give away my power to other people and circumstances. So, I tried these empowering responses:

I WANT SOMETHING BETTER
I DESERVE SOMETHING BETTER
THIS DOESN'T WORK FOR ME
I LOVE YOU, BUT I NEED SOMETHING MORE
I WANT TO DO THIS INSTEAD
I DON'T WANT TO SETTLE FOR SECOND BEST

I wasn't happy, so I had to stand up and say something. Walk through my fear, the discomfort, the smallness. Take a stand. Do it for myself.

I didn't have to have it all figured out. And, I knew that it might not all come together overnight. But I had to align myself with becoming the best version of me. I had to start to trust in the connection I had to myself.

I am capable of making smart, empowered and aligned decisions! No matter what anyone from my past or present has told me!

I had to feel it all in my body. Feel where in my life I was settling…

Loneliness on Your Path
(2019)

As you're moving along your spiritual journey or a new path in life, it's common to have feelings of loneliness arise.

You know you're not who you used to be, and yet you're still feeling into the person you're becoming.

The things that you used to enjoy, fall flat now.

Conversations that aren't soulful feel effortful.

You start to outgrow relationships.

I've learned to lean into this uncomfortable middle space and do whatever I need to do to protect my energy and preserve my sanity.

This means I'm on the right path!

The Universe is lining up to support my growth in a big way, by eliminating the people, the beliefs and the things that are no longer in alignment with this new me.

So, it's okay to move on.

It's okay to not return that call or text message.

It's okay to unfriend someone on social media, or even get off social media!

It's okay to distance yourself from family.

It's okay to say no to anything not serving your highest good!

I will come up against resistance. People who don't want to change, don't like to see anyone else grow and evolve. But it's not personal! It's just where they are in their evolution.

I just keep doing me.

I am magnificent, and my growth is beautiful!

I am not alone!

I see me. I feel me. I hear me. I support me!

I am calling in my inner Spiritual Gangster and getting back to work! I am here to make a difference, and I am divine.

Enlightenment
(2019)

When I was nineteen, I thought that to achieve enlightenment, I had to give up all material possessions, give up my name and my world as I knew it. That's how the spiritual world looked twenty years ago from my perspective.

So that's what I did.

For nearly eight years, I was a monk, or meditation student/teacher. I wore only white clothing, gave up my English name and all worldly possessions.

I was then given a Sanskrit name, Sri Lakshmi, by my Teacher during a sacred ceremony. I was Sri for short.

I meditated anywhere between six and eighteen hours a day.

It was an interesting time in my life, but looking back, it was a time when I gave away most of my power. I gave away my personal power to people I thought were at a higher level of consciousness. People I thought knew better than I did about what I needed and wanted.

Through trying to lose my identity and sense of self, I also lost what made me, ME. I lost the shine in my personality, all in the name of achieving "enlightenment."

And now twelve years, after leaving that part of my journey, I can truly say I experience more joy, peace and freedom than I ever did trying to meditate "myself" away.

I still have times I sit down and meditate, but I also experience accessing a deeper inner well of knowing through dance and movement.

I have more "peak" experiences hiking through the mountains and exploring foreign countries.

I've come to understand that it's not about trying to rid myself of all thought, but about changing my reaction to them.

That's where true peace comes from.

So, here I am, full of color, loving the name I was given the day I was born into this physical reality, and I have worldly possessions I treasure immensely.

I am doing whatever brings me peace, joy and freedom!

That's how I'm raising my consciousness.

Change the story!
(2019)

Why was I insisting on replaying the story of my life, over and over, in a way that didn't feel empowering, but in a way that was keeping me stuck in my stories?

I don't have to!

When I was going through my divorce five years ago, a family member used to always refer to my "track record in life."

At the time, I was in such a messy place within myself, that I allowed those words to consume me for several years, and I started to believe in whatever "track record" this person thought I had.

I suppose they saw my "bad decisions," and felt as though they had the right to judge me and make me feel as though I'd always made bad decisions.

Over the past year, I made the conscious choice to re-write my story. I decided to look back on my "track record," with gentleness, forgiveness and grace.

And I wrote myself a new story. One of resilience, strength and empowerment.

I decided the only person's opinion about my life I need to worry about at the end of the day is mine. I'm the only one who gets to write my story, in whatever way I want.

My story, flaws and all, struggles and heartbreak, love and loss.

There's perfection in all of it.

I have no shame for my life, and the experiences I've gone through. And because of that, I get to be happy and free.

So, would I rather spend my time worrying about what other people think, or owning my story...my beautiful, perfect and magical TRACK RECORD?

I get to choose!

The Pause
(2019)

The moment when you naturally want to react but instead take a conscious step back.

Reaction isn't always a negative response.

I can let excitement get the best of me, because I'm a positive person, and I find life utterly fascinating and exciting.

Opportunities present themselves, and my natural reaction is to say "yes!" to everything.

However, excitement does not always equal alignment.

This past weekend at our retreat, we talked a lot about The Pause – how in each moment of interaction with another being, it's in our best interest to pause, reflect and be conscious of how we respond or react.

Not everything needs an answer now.

Not everything needs a response now.

By taking that moment, you allow the feelings in your body to be your guide. They are your compass, leading you to your own True North, your truth.

I allow yourself to open to what's in alignment and for my highest good, and what's not. Every opportunity that's presented to me has a gift, if I am open to receiving the messages.

And it's in the stillness, the silence, The Pause, where I am best able to hear the messages clearly.

I am getting comfortable with the sometimes uncomfortable pause!

Flying
(2019)

You know what's interesting about flying?

We basically hop inside this metal capsule looking thingy and speed our way through the sky!

And part of the process is having to completely surrender and give up control.

We have no idea whether or not we'll make it to our destination. We pray for the best, and then we let go.

Sometimes our journey is smooth sailing. And sometimes we experience turbulence, with bumps along the way.

But when we're on a plane, there is nothing we can do.

We have to sit back, relax and attempt to enjoy ourselves as much as we can. We might close our eyes, praying for it to be over. We might be full of energy, rocking out to an awesome playlist and getting inspired. Or maybe we're somewhere in between, not sure how we feel yet.

The thing is we get to choose whether we enjoy the ride or not. It's our choice.

Doesn't this kinda sound like a metaphor for life?!

As much as we want to control our journeys, we can't.

Life will always throw us curveballs.

But it's our choice as to how we react to them.

We decide whether we're going to resist or surrender to wherever the wind blows.

Soak in and feel the magic of this Spotify Playlist I created for Crystal Clear:

https://open.spotify.com/user/1265771279/playlist/7megvS8Z0q JGEyvFi3Um9p?si=-4lk7ceARwyZO7xazlgeUA

Chapter 7

The

Kelsey

Show

2.0

The Kelsey Show 2.0 is the part of the show where I just know. I know who I am, what I'm here to do and who I'm here to be...and that's me. I'm here to keep dancing along these adventures of awakening, understanding there's no destination. There's no end to this game.

And that's so freeing!

There will always be shadows. Life will always be a bit messy. And I've come to a place where I've embraced the dance. I have a new depth of understanding that I'm this infinite, spiritual being, and yet, I'm also a human being, who's here to experience and feel everything I possibly can. And it's in the messiness, that my magic medicine comes to life.

I've alchemized my past pains into personal power, and now, I get to be my fiery, fierce, smart and sassy self.

So, how will I continue this dance?

Using the mile markers I've placed all along the road map of my journey. Mile markers such as: Knowing you're in the right place, Knowing there's no right or wrong decision, Knowing you've got to have fun, Being high on life, Embodying that high, Using nature's medicine, Making space for stillness...and more...

Join me and let's dance!

You're in the right place if…

You've spent your life wandering and wondering
You have insatiable wanderlust, but don't know where to start
You're looking to have a travel experience with meaning
You're searching for deeper meaning in life
You like to read about synchronicities and coincidences
You'd like to learn how to hone-in on your intuition
You'd like to step out of your travel box
You'd like tools to bring the sacred into your everyday experience
You're searching for deeper meaning in your life
You want to feel inspired by travel
You're a lightworker, sensitive to energies
If you love crystals, sage and all the witchy things
Are looking for a daily spiritual practice
If you'd like to connect more with your body
If you'd like to remember your essence is wise, wild and free
You want to trust yourself more
You want to embody your feminine essence
You want to find answers inside by going outside
You'd like to escape the culture of doing more, faster, better
You'd like help moving through life with meaning
You'd like to engage in ritual, pilgrimage and community connections to open your heart, mind and spirit
You'd like to shift your perspective from going through the motions to savoring life as sacred
You'd like to have more intuition-led travel experiences
You want to learn how to find the magic in the mundane
You'd like to tap into your true essence through movement
You're looking to heal or are on a healing journey
You want to experience more authenticity
You'd like a map to accessing more joy, freedom and authenticity

You'd like priceless tools and practices to reconnect with your innate intelligence and sense of knowing what is right for you

You'd like to celebrate your journey

You'd like to live a life filled with peace, passion and purpose

You'd like to feel positively empowered

What if I told you there was no
"right" or "wrong" decision in life?

There's just a decision. And one might get you to your goal/destination more quickly, but it doesn't always mean it's a "better" decision. It just is.

We get so caught up in doing things "right." Fear emerges to trap us in a space of wrong doing, of feeling as though we are going to fail. But there is no failure!

If something doesn't happen the way you want it to, there's usually a reason, which isn't currently apparent. It may take days, weeks, months or even years to grasp, but someday you'll look back and see the perfection in it all.

I used to get in my head, listening to family members discuss my "poor decisions," or even better...my "track record" in life. I used to cry and be angry, so concerned over what other people were thinking about me, especially my family.

And now it's laughable. Because we all have a track record! We have ALL made decisions that maybe didn't look "right" on the outside to anyone else.

But it's your path. Sometimes the path you take will be alone, sometimes you'll have support. But either way, it's the right way….for you.

When teaching Qoya, we say there's no way to do it wrong. And the way you know you're doing it right is when it feels true in your body.

What if we could live our lives in such a way?

Are we having fun yet?

It's come to my attention that I need to have more fun. What?! Me??

Yep. It's time to shake things up. I'm really good at shaking and stirring things up for everyone else, and it's now time for my own soul-stirring.

Wild, untamed Kelsey is ready to come back out. You probably didn't notice she went anywhere, but I've been feeling it.

I've thrown myself into my work and building my business this year full-on because doing things full-on is my personality. I don't half-ass anything.

However, my playtime has been neglected, so it's time to ease up a bit and start playing more.

And my self-care practices are not what I consider play! I've got the daily rituals that keep me tapped in and present, but I'm hungry for something more.

Less than 24 hours away from home has opened up my heart and mind to so much that was feeling stagnant back home.

This is exactly why travel has always been a priority in my life!

So, I'm feeling into my creative play space in my hotel room, and I'm ready for what's coming over the next few days.

This trip has stirred my soul in a massive way!

Even when you have your daily rituals and are consistently showing up for yourself and the world, it's still a good idea to shake things up!

And that's exactly my gift to the world...making waves.

Appreciation

I'm a mover, shaker, risk-taker and magic maker!

And this past weekend, we embodied all of that and more as our incredible group of women celebrated life to the fullest!

I've returned from this trip with so much gold and appreciation for the conscious connections I have all around me.

High on Life

I'm a magical, mystical mo-fo who's stepping into my next level of spiritual gifts and personal power.

I see fairies, ghosts and spirits, I hear voices and clear messages, I channel, have visions, sense energies and beings around me, and I'm having a freaking blast!

I've discovered how to feel high AF from simply being me and doing the things that light me up, without using anything external to alter my state of mind.

There's a time and place for everything, but I'm here to tell you that you don't need any "medicine" other than your own, to expand your awareness and tap into higher and deeper states of consciousness.

You simply need an open mind, heart and guidance!

Do you know how many people reach out to share their mystical experiences with me because they've never felt comfortable to share with anyone else?!

It's time we all feel seen, heard, understood and celebrated for our uniqueness!

Embody the High

I got into the world of self-development and drugs around the same time...when I was fourteen after a suicide attempt and several months in the hospital.

I decided that if I couldn't physically leave this world, I would at least do what I could to leave my body and explore what else was going on out there in the cosmos.

For years, I excelled at exploring other realms and the depths of consciousness, however, the lows that would occur after the highs grew increasingly more painful.

There were never enough drugs. There was never enough meditation time (even at eighteen hours a day). I found euphoria through sex and even rope bondage (yes, consensual pain can actually be a very spiritual experience).

I did anything to chase the high...exercise, sex work, hiking way past my physical limits.

These things aren't all negative. There's nothing wrong with wanting the experience of oneness, bliss and unity. That's the truth of who we are.

But those things aren't feelings or emotions. They're states of being.

And what I've learned to cultivate over the past 25 years on my adventure of awakening is how to maintain a state of bliss no matter what's going on externally.

I see a whole lot of self-development out there but not enough consciousness conversations, so that's what I'm here to bring!

Nature's Medicine

I tried to chase the sunset home, but I didn't make it. The clouds tonight were bright pink and so inviting I wanted to float away!

Mother recently reminded me how much I hated the outdoors as a child, and now, I see myself in my daughter. It's hard to imagine myself like that as now I embrace every moment in nature that I get.

Nature grounds me and quiets my mind...every time. I used to always wear headphones when I walked or hiked, but now, I walk in silence and encourage others to do the same.

It's in the silence you hear the messages you're desiring to receive...from the plants, animals, birds, water, trees and spirit.

Fill yourself up with Mama Earth's medicine!

If you're feeling lost, confused or disconnected, go outside and walk or sit in silence. You might notice you don't feel quite so alone.

**Ahhh...the phases of the moon
mirror the phases of life**

Today, I'm praying for a friend whose son recently passed and for another friend who's anxiously awaiting the arrival of her new son!

Potent energies abound!

Don't forget to sloooow down and honor your own rhythmic cycles of creation and destruction.

Highly Grounded

Wouldn't it be cool if you could take all those mystical "out there" experiences you have and ground them into your daily life?

As if you could experience life as nothing other than complete magic!

For me, oneness and non-duality feel as if I'm almost pulled to the center of the Earth. As if the bottom drops out, and there's everything and nothing, all at once.

When I lived within an intentional community, we'd share our experiences of this every night, and I did that for eight years! Can you imagine?!

How often do you get to have conscious conversations like that?

This isn't just basic awareness talk or Law of Attraction. This is going into the depths.

It's a cross between Warrior and Monk.

Wanna get high and grounded simultaneously?

Do you actually meditate or make space for stillness?

So many people come to me saying they can't meditate when what they're doing is sitting for about sixty seconds, getting frustrated they're still having thoughts and can't quiet them and then give up.

Meditation is a practice, like yoga or any other kind of exercise. It's an exercise for your mind. The more you practice it, the more you'll strengthen your meditation muscle. It takes sitting still through the discomfort and allowing your nervous system to chill out.

It's not believing that you have to "eliminate" all your thoughts.

I'm finding it more and more fascinating how many "spiritual" people I know can hardly ever sit still.

And with social media, it's even more important now that we take time every day, without distraction and noise clouding our own judgment and preventing divine downloads.

If you want to tap into your spiritual gifts and psychic abilities, it's paramount you allow yourself the space to do so.

Are you all in?

I'm not a dip my toe in and test the waters kind of gal. When I'm in, I go all in and to the depths.

Can you relate?

Last week, a friend commented on how I'm always "on." I found that curious and explored what that meant to me…

It's the depth of my hunger and the drive that keeps me alive. It's the fire and magic in my belly. It's being so present, at peace and needing absolutely nothing, while at the same time knowing I am and can have everything.

It's unwavering dedication to explore the adventures of awakening and create soul stirrings within all whom I encounter. It's feeling high on life but rooted in Mama Earth simultaneously.

Are you ready to go all in? To explore the depths of consciousness and beyond...

Would you like to have fun while strengthening your spiritual gifts and abilities, and make an impact simply by being you?

Sunsets

It's virtually impossible for me to be discontent while watching the sunset and the transition from daylight to nighttime. It's my most magical time of day.

Does anyone else avidly obsess about sunsets and chase them around the world?

Spiritual Gifts

We all have spiritual gifts, and what's funny is that once you discover what those gifts are, you'll realize you've known for a long time, and you'll wonder how you didn't "get it" sooner.

And that's because you had to wander down your own unique path of self-discovery and arrive at each destination at just the right time.

If you feel like it's time to dig a little deeper and hone-in on what your spiritual gifts, psychic powers and magic medicine are, you're in the right place!

One of my gifts is to stir your soul. To dive in and honor the conversations you don't even know you're craving. To awaken parts of yourself lying dormant, ready to rise again.

When you're ready, I'm here for you. And even if you're not ready, I'm here holding the space until you decide to embark on the journey your soul has been calling you to take.

But here's the thing...we have today. That's it. Our dream futures that we all obsessively think about and imagine being our reality can exist right now! So, why not make today the day you said yes to your amazingness and have today be the day everything changed?

Obsessed

That used to be a dirty word.
OCD.
A "diagnosis" I decided to not let define me.
Passionate, fiery, hungry.
That's me.
I've never gotten what I wanted by halfway wanting it.
I never traveled around the world by sitting at home wishing I was traveling.
I never made a better life for myself by wishing my life would miraculously get better.
I didn't change my belief systems and habits by hoping they'd change themselves overnight.
Nope.
It's my *obsession* with deeper knowledge and expanding awareness.
It's my *hunger* for magic and endlessly epic days.
It's my *passion* for truth and igniting the *fiery* truth in others.
How far are you willing to go?
What are you willing to leave behind?
Who are you ready to be?
It's time to step out of the illusion and into illumination.
It's time to set aside your crystals, oracle cards and sage.
It's time for you to become the Oracle!
It's time for you to Trust in your abilities.
It's time for you to Know who you are and What you came here to do!
You don't need anything outside of you.
You don't need plant medicine.
You don't need psychic readings.
You don't need distractions.
You need to be authentically inspired to be you, in all your cosmic glory!

Today I was given a beautiful gift

The gift of peace.
The gift of non-duality.
The gift of choice.
Today I could've spun out.
I could've gone into stories and judgment.
I could've reacted.
Instead, I was given the beautiful gift of choosing to remember who I am.
To remain in stillness and peace in even the direst circumstances.
The gift of trust.
When Spirit whispered in my ear and said, "Do you trust?" And I said, "Of course."
And then I heard again, "Do you really trust?"
I got even more still and this time I felt it in bones when I answered, "Yes, I trust."
The magic that occurred at that moment changed everything. So much so that it's still settling into my body.
An even deeper knowing that the Universe is always in my favor.
A new depth of complete and utter gratitude for the understanding of the interconnectedness of everything and everyone.
My loves, we are resourceful AF.
We are pure consciousness.
We are meant to be in community and help one another.
If you're a spiritual being who's afraid to ask for help and afraid to receive, you're living in duality. And no matter what you achieve or how much money you make, you'll still experience everything as being outside of yourself.
There will always be waves at the beach. That's part of its beauty. But you get to choose whether you want to ride those

waves or let them pull you under. Either way, you always were and always will be the beach itself.

Don't forget how infinite, vast and powerful you are.

Would you like to explore the depths with me?

Tonight brought an unexpected
ending to a chapter in my life

It became crystal clear to me over the past few days that my time of teaching *Qoya* at my local studio space for the past 2 1/2 years was coming to a close.

My *Qoya* wingspan is growing far and wide, and it's time to expand into the vision for *Qoya* that's always been in my heart.

I can't say enough about how much I appreciate taking my very first *Qoya* class at this studio, doing my practice classes there and then going on to become a certified teacher, leading countless sacred women's circles in that space, with several other *Qoya* teachers whom I deeply respect.

Qoya has been one of the most deeply profound spiritual practices I've ever come across and is part of my daily practice.

Sisterhood for me has become everything...my lifeline, sacred bonds and support.

I will continue teaching private group classes and pop up classes around Indianapolis, as well as at workshops, retreats and even online!

This is the natural evolution, and although this was absolutely not planned, it feels completely perfect.

I have several more chapters of my life closing in the coming weeks, and as I'm continually expanding and growing, I hadn't thought about what would need to fall away to make room for this expansion.

I honor the process and embrace the adventure!

Stop apologizing and take up space!

The last few mornings, I woke up with a deep desire to be hiking in the woods, so I've followed the call each day to my local state park.

For an added feeling of seclusion and magic, I frequently hike along the bike trails as there's not as much foot traffic.

When the bikes pass by, I move over out of the way, as is necessary, and I've noticed a trend.

The men pass by and say, "Thank you." The women pass by and say, "I'm sorry."

My beautiful sisters, why are we always apologizing?

We apologize for taking up space, for making noise, for feeling, for receiving support, for our mere existence!

And it's time we stop.

It's time we allow our energy to take up space!

It's time we physically go where we want.

It's time we're loud, boisterous and excited without hesitation.

Unless you've truly done someone wrong that requires a genuine apology, please release the "I'm sorry." You don't have to apologize for being you!

#sorrynotsorry

Does where you live affect your happiness?

This has been a theme amongst my Indiana soul family and blood family in the past week or so.

My mother, brother and I have been swapping stories about our 5 to 10-year plans, which include being anywhere other than Indiana.

And my soul family and I have been sharing our deep-rooted desires to be in the mountains or deserts and what it's like to *feel* bound to a physical location we don't sense a deep connection to.

It's easy to feel inspired when you can drive to the ocean on a whim, hike mountaintops or stargaze in the desert. Even big cities have the hustle and bustle energy that can feel intoxicating. But when you're a wild child, free-spirited lightworker living in Indiana, it can feel like a real challenge at times.

So, what I say is that adventure is a state of mind!

I *chose* to move back to Indiana twelve years ago, and I *chose* to have a child here, and I'm lucky her dad actually wants her in his life.

My soul *chose* to experience many challenges in this lifetime. I was never meant for the easy road, however, that doesn't mean I can't be at ease no matter where I am.

It takes courage to find the magic and light when it's not so obvious.

It takes dedication to go within to the unchanging when your outer circumstances aren't what you desire.

And it takes *choosing* to experience peace, joy and inspiration no matter what because all of that ultimately comes from inside.

There's beauty and magic everywhere if we only open our eyes.

So, does where you live affect your happiness? That's up to you!

Life is one big adventure, and it's what we choose to make of it!

P.S. I do have a pretty stellar lake view...just sayin'...

Who you surround yourself with is everything

Go where you're celebrated.

Be with people who see you as your highest possible self.

The ones who inspire you to be authentically you.

Sometimes, it blows my mind how many incredible women I'm calling into my circle, and other times it's more, "Of course I am."

That's my life every day...in flow and in awe. That's what magic is!

The more you share of yourself genuinely, and the more you align with your highest truth, the more you'll attract others who also align with you and your vision.

I have women reach out to me regularly who are desperate for connection, for friendship and sisterhood...and they don't know how to get it.

My advice is this:

1. Stay intentional
2. Do the inner work that's keeping you from manifesting those relationships
3. Be patient

True connections are a balance of giving and receiving.

They will show up when you decide to show up! As the saying goes...you can only meet others as deeply as you've met yourself.

If you're craving deeper, more soulful and heart-centered conversations and connections, it starts with you.

Are you addicted to your trauma?

Trauma = Drama

Now, before you think I'm not being sympathetic, let me explain...
I've experienced a lot of trauma in my life, including:

- ✓ childhood sexual abuse
- ✓ surviving a dramatic suicide attempt
- ✓ emotional abuse
- ✓ verbal abuse
- ✓ physical abuse
- ✓ drug abuse
- ✓ rape
- ✓ being mindfucked in a spiritual cult for eight years
- ✓ financial abuse
- ✓ narcissism
- ✓ extreme gaslighting
- ✓ a man who made babies with other women while being married to me...

...the list goes on and on.

So, I have just about as much empathy as is humanly possible.

But...something really shifted in me the past few years, especially through the creation of my autobiography.

I carried my stories of trauma for years...about thirty to be exact. And not only did I carry them, but I also rehearsed them, I played with them, I fostered the feelings that came along with them.

I did this because I didn't know who I was without the trauma, without the stories and the drama that came with them.

They were comfortable. They allowed me to stay small, to maintain my identity as the victim and to be able to make excuses for my actions and behavior...because, you know, "trauma."

But I always knew I was more than that! I always knew that someday I wouldn't be defined by what I went through. That I'd be defined by who I am and who I've become.

We *need* to share our stories. They need to be released from the shadows and surrendered to the light.

I'm the biggest advocate for that, and soon, every thought, from all my years of trauma, will be released out into the world. (In fact, you've been reading all about them throughout this book.) The only way that was possible is because I don't identify with those parts of myself anymore. They've all taken a backseat.

I understand in a deeply profound way that my soul chose to have those experiences in this lifetime. Just as my daughter's soul has. And just as your soul has, too.

Even in the midst of the chaos and trauma, somewhere deep inside a hunger for truth has always been ravenous, and an uncontrollable fire has burned. I just had to learn to harness that energy in a different way. And when I did, I was able to alchemize my pain into personal empowerment.

So, tell your stories. Live and speak your truth. Rise above the chaos and the noise. And then settle into the juicy peace, stillness and joy that is your birthright no matter what you've been through!

I'm not a trauma survivor. My goal was never to merely survive.

I'm a liver and lover of this game called life. When we understand that we're all just perfectly playing our parts, we'll truly be free.

That doesn't mean we aren't human, with human emotions. I still have mine intact. And I bet you do, too.

And yet, even in the midst of emotion, there's something beautiful and unwavering. With every breakdown, comes a breaking open. The universe is not conspiring against us. We're being led, being guided deeper into the truth of who we are.

There were days, weeks and months I wanted it all to end. Times that felt excruciatingly endless. Days where I couldn't function, nights that were terrorizing.

And yet, somehow, I made it through, and you made it, too. And…we're still here.

Now, when I'm having a bad moment, I appreciate the worst moments I ever had because it puts it all into perspective.

Remember the love you thought would break you?

Remember the addiction you thought you'd never beat?

Remember when you swore you'd never open up again, but then you did?

It's time we celebrate all we've overcome and celebrate that we're here today!

Let's allow our souls to stir and our hearts to be broken open. We're being guided to alchemize that pain and live a life of pure joy and love!

"Ohhh...you're THE mover and shaker, huh?"

This is what I heard upon being introduced to someone this morning through mutual friends. And I've heard various versions of this from many people over the past week.

Apparently, my reputation now proceeds me.

Yep, I like to stir things up! Not forcefully or willfully, just by being me.

My presence and energy have a way of inviting you to come out and play! It piques curiosity. It's fire and light. Calm and bright.

Nothing is stagnant in the world of The Kelsey Show 2.0, and I'm shaking things up in a big way.

Sacred Connection (2019)

In about 36 hours, I'll be en route to the red rocks of Sedona.

And in my preparations, I'm overcome with such immense gratitude for everything in my life that's led up to this point in time.

Those moments when you can reflect on all the struggles, the pain and the darkness I wasn't sure I would ever emerge from, feeling nothing but grateful for all of it.

I wouldn't change a thing, because it all led me here, to living out my soul's purpose.

It's led me to share my stories and gifts with beautiful souls who are trusting me to guide them as they discover their own paths.

And this Sacred Connection Retreat is just the beginning!

My year ahead is mapped out with more retreats, mentorship programs and so much MAGIC, I can hardly contain it all.

And it's all been so much easier because of the incredible support I've received from friends, mentors, coaches, connections, synchronicities and people I don't even know personally!

The messages and texts I received in support of this journey to Arizona have my heart overflowing.

I've even had several amazing women bless me with gifts for my retreat participants! You guys, how blessed am I?! It makes me cry tears of joy.

Thank you, THANK YOU.

To all those who have supported my journey through the years, and to those who haven't. They've all made me stronger and able to stand with more confidence and conviction.

This might be my first hosted destination retreat, but I've already done it a hundred times across many lifetimes and realities!

My magic has just begun to unfold, and I'm looking forward to its continual unfolding.

Best laid plans

There's no way to truly ever know where we're going to end up. Even the best-laid plans have a way of turning upside down.

That's why I've spent the last few years focusing on how I want to *feel* instead of the details of what I want to do or where I want to be.

Those things are continually evolving and shifting, as am I.

However, when I focus on how I want to *feel*, I trust that I will end up where I desire to be, no matter how it looks.

Right now, I have big, wild dreams, but three years ago…this, right here, where I am, right now, was my big wild dream!

And three years ago, when I embarked on my first solo travel adventure to the magical land of Iceland for ten days, I had no idea that every page of my journal I wrote in my Airbnb back then would now be getting published in my first book.

Raw, unfiltered and unedited.

Can you imagine having all your thoughts, feelings and musings laid out for the world to see?

Have you ever done something you never imagined you could do and then, when you did, it felt so natural and ordinary?

How would it feel to realize you actually *are* the person you want to be?

Soul Stirring

I like to stir the pot.
In a way that ignites the fire within you.
To wake you up and shake you up.
To help you remember the magic.
To inspire your wildest dreams and motivate you to be more.
I like to rattle cages.
To wake up the dormant parts of you.
To show you another way.
To help you embrace ALL of you.
I like to make waves.
To teach you how to flow.
To guide you through your growth.
To awaken you to the adventure.

Soak in and feel the magic of this Spotify Playlist I created for The Kelsey Show 2.0:

https://open.spotify.com/user/1265771279/playlist/2dzvzrS9eMS 1ySe3WKclY7?si=eemnzOcjQ0aZGRpWPOha4g

Conclusion

Phew. We made it! We journeyed together through the first book of the Adventures of Awakening! You witnessed my story, my pain and my process of alchemizing my pain into personal empowerment. And I've only just begun!

I'm looking forward to diving even deeper into the delicious dance of the shadows in the next book. Together, we'll explore the diaries of my days as a BDSM bunny and how I alchemized my shadows in very unconventional ways.

We're all unique creatures, and my hope is to bring a voice to those who hide in the shadows of sex fetishes and sex work and normalize these conversations.

To create spaces where those with untold stories can gather and release the traumas from their bodies. To be a safe space holder for those ready to release their past, release judgment and fear and move into a place of freedom and empowerment.

If you'd like to discover how to dance with your own shadows, share your untold stories of abuse, abortion, rape or trauma, and gather in sacred sisterhood, I invite you to connect with me at www.thekelseydecker.com. There, you can also subscribe to my mailing list and get all the details on my next adventures of awakening!

Appendix

A

My Journey (Iceland)

(Note: The following are my actual, unedited diary entries from my trip to Iceland, February 2017)

I'm sitting alone in my dark, quiet, quaint little Airbnb and I'm very aware of just how alone I am. I went out to dinner tonight and had a delightful meal at Tapas Barrin in Reyjavik. It was a small, upscale, nicely decorated restaurant and I was totally digging the ambiance.

As I sat there, memories of my life kept flashing by. That's been happening a lot lately. It reminds me of Liz's experiences in Eat Pray Love. I think this happens because these things come up to be healed and leave the body.

I was enjoying my meal and flashed back to the last time *he* and I went out for tapas. I was so on edge and anxious. And I realized that the loneliest times I've ever spent weren't when I was alone. I've always felt most alone within relationships. That's a sad realization.

As much as I grieve the good times, especially with him, I don't miss how miserable I felt the rest of the time. And it's always been like that. I'm not sure what it feels like any other way.

Being with others makes me feel so alone, so misunderstood. Is it because I've never quite understood myself?

The Blue Lagoon was magical. I kinda wish I hadn't been so jet-lagged so I could remember it more. Surreal is the perfect word. And you know what? I sat in that water taking photos, soaking it all in and watching the most stunning sunrise of my life and as I looked around, I was surrounded by couples intertwined in each other's bodies. And I actually felt happy for them.

If I felt any sadness in missing *him*, it was only momentary and passed so quickly I hardly remember. I was meant to be there alone. And I'm still happy to be here alone. I might just get addicted to this solo travel thing.

I've met exactly 4 women traveling to Iceland alone so far. Well, one was actually in transit to Denmark, but it's been nice talking to each one of them briefly.

I saw another woman sitting alone at dinner tonight, but she didn't seem to want to be bothered. And then another one after her at the same table.

• • •

I'm really starting to wonder what on earth has happened to my libido, charm and charisma. I don't seem to be attracting men into my life or they hardly seem to glance in my direction.

It must be some kind of vibe I'm giving off, or not giving off. I'm not sure. I feel so utterly introverted and yet I can sense somewhere in there is a seductress that wants to get out. She shined for a brief moment tonight.

I think the waiter at the restaurant was talking about me. He kept smiling every time he passed my table and then all the waiters were talking. I was slightly disappointed he wasn't around when I left. That would've been fun.

There was another guy at the Blue Lagoon today too. He was obviously there alone and there weren't many of us by ourselves. He swam up close to me several times and just waited, but never made a move.

I became incredibly anxious about how terrible I looked and felt, having just gotten off my red-eye flight from the States. I was sleep and food-deprived and had the biggest black bags and circles around my eyes, I'd ever seen. So I convinced myself that when he got close, he realized how wretched I was and swam away.

I'd also seen him talking with several other groups of people and he was endlessly drinking beer in the hot water. Boy was he looking good though.

I decided the last thing I wanted during my peacefulness at the lagoon was to be worrying about some stupid guy who means nothing really. Or be worrying about what anybody was thinking about me. It's none of my business anyway.

I thought for sure I was going to get here and be all hot and bothered and ready to get back out there and at least get laid. But somewhat disappointingly, I feel quite the opposite. The shower in my Airbnb even has one of those nice shower heads that can be used for "special" purposes, but even that had no appeal tonight during my shower.

Maybe I'm just tired. Or maybe I'm physically tired and tired of always making things about a man.

I don't want to be the bitter, single woman though. The one that wants nothing to do with men. Someday it will be nice again, but I don't see it any time soon. I don't think anyone can quite understand how much and how badly I need this time to myself. Time to really reflect.

And who knows, maybe in a few days I'll feel differently. Everything is always changing. I feel like I could write a book all night, but I need to sleep. I'm hoping to attempt going to Snaefellsnes tomorrow.

• • •

One more thing I'll say is that traveling alone is not for the faint of heart and not for the directionally challenged. I was patting myself on the back tonight as I found my way back to the house through the snow, in the dark a couple different times.

I remembered how I've always had a knack for directions. And I can easily retrace my steps, especially when I'm alone and not distracted by someone or something else. It was very impressive tonight. I had a moment where I wanted someone to say "Wow Kelsey, that was amazing. You're so good at that." But I just said it out loud to myself instead. haha

I can't believe this is my first night here. I feel like so much has happened already. Well, that's my life though. I even went grocery shopping today and I'm all set to cook. We'll see what more is in store for the rest of this trip.

• • •

My glacier hike was canceled due to weather, but they rescheduled it for Saturday. It's funny I'm not even upset. Maybe I can go to Elf School now!

I'm having an indecisive day. One part of me loves being all alone in this little cottage and yet part of me feels I should be "doing" something. The weather is very bad. The roads in and out of the city have all been closed. Apparently that's a pretty big deal.

So I spent time on my phone figuring out if it's okay to leave the house. I like that when I'm not here in the house, I have no cell service or wifi. I hate this phone and my mindless addiction to it. At least I've spent my time being quiet. I'm tired. So tired. I wonder if I'll ever stop being tired.

My health is my priority when I get home. That's been glaringly obvious to me. I'm loving how my body looks right now, except for my hallowed face. I've lost so much weight, but I don't like how it feels. I'm tired beyond exhaustion. It's no wonder I can't think straight. And this time zone change certainly doesn't help.

I love how crisp and white this room is. And the perfect amount of light during the day, coupled with complete darkness at night. It's a perfect size too. A lovely choice.

I keep staring at the dress I have hanging. I do hope I get the chance to wear it. This weather really is throwing things off. Not necessarily in a bad way. Hell, I'm in Iceland in February. But it's still throwing my plans off. I think I'll go to Elf School in an hour. That sounds charming and delightful. And then I can see if this evening brings about any fun.

I'm feeling anxious to meet people and let loose. I've been feeling peaceful for the most part, but I miss having fun. I need that. I need to feel like that part of me isn't gone forever. I want to feel desired and wanted. I miss *him*. Not all the icky bits, but the way he used to look at me.

I slept in yesterday morning. I had planned to do the Snaefellsnes Peninsula, but my body needed sleep. I slept until 9:30 am and then didn't get out of bed until 10:00 am. By then I decided I didn't want to rush and I'd missed a couple of houses of precious daylight already so I opted for the Golden Circle Tour.

I learned a lot about myself doing that tour. As I drove out of the city and saw the blanket of white and all the surrounding mountains, I started to cry. It was so magnificent. The GPS in my upgraded car has been priceless and has taken me everywhere with ease.

The first stop was Pingvellir National Park. It was really crowded with tourists, which I found myself unimpressed and slightly annoyed with. Yesterday made me see how much I loathe tourist destinations. I prefer doing what the locals do. I thought about that and how everywhere I've ever traveled there's been an insecurity of not wanting to look or seem like a tourist. I thought it was a confidence issue, but perhaps that's not it at all. I'm not sure yet.

After that, I went to the famous Geysir. Along the way, there were tourists pulled off into lots to take beautiful pictures. This didn't appeal to me. Because I was alone or because it was just another scenery shot? I'm not sure about that either.

Then I started seeing the pretty ponies! OMG, they were so adorable! I kept thinking about our secretary at work because she was obsessed with me seeing the ponies.

There were 2 cars pulled off at one point and I was flabbergasted at how unsafe they were being for the other cars. "Damn tourists", I thought. Then a couple of miles later there wasn't anyone else around and a car was on the side of the road with girls petting the horses. I said the hell with it and pulled over. I got two quick pics and sure enough, a policeman pulled over and we got chastised for being unsafe. Figures!

• • •

This is heaven. I'm splurging on a fancy expensive meal which might be my last meal out. Oh, how the time flies. I scored and got a window seat that I requested when the last table left. I'm in the Old Harbor area of town, looking out on the harbor. There's a whale-watching boat about to leave. Or actually I'm thinking it's probably a Northern Lights Tour. Not going to have much luck tonight. Chances aren't looking good. The next two nights are looking *very* good for me! I'm considering booking a tour for Tuesday night.

This heater right beside me feels heavenly. The cold is finally getting to me. More like the record-breaking snowfall we got last night. I had to shovel my car out of 8 feet of snow today and it was a total riot. I actually somewhat enjoyed it and felt very accomplished at the end. I loved the flea and food market this morning as it was my kind of place.

This is peace right here. The candlelight and the lights of the harbor. If only the guy a few tables over would keep it down. It's the same peaceful feeling I get being out on the open road. I'm so glad I did that today. It's so funny how I really have not wanted to interact with anyone.

• • •

And just like that, it ends. I'm sitting on a flight back to the States and I look over to see the last glimpse of white mountains. If I wasn't on a plane I would break down crying.

The airport was stressful. It jolted me back. Back to what, I'm not sure. Keflavik is a lovely airport with a great food area that I didn't have time to explore. They sure get you at the duty-free stores though. I don't know what came over me but somehow I ended up with $75 worth of white chocolate, only found in Iceland, all kinds of gluten-free licorice and even some jelly beans, I'm super excited about! Since when do I eat candy?

"It's for my daughter," I told myself. Hahaha. Yeah right. I can hear her agreeing with the fact that she knows I'll eat it all. God, I miss her. Like I really miss her now. I just want to wrap my arms around her and hold her forever. Why is that when I'm "home" I feel lonely and when I travel never feel that way?

I *am* getting anxious for some human interaction though. But the tricky part of that is I only feel like talking to someone that's been to Iceland, who would really understand the withdrawal from that magical world.

I ended up bringing back a couple of packs of smoked lamb and a variety of cheeses, as well as some rice crackers coated in chocolate for my daughter. Since when do I eat meat and cheese?

I went to the Whales Museum before I left for the airport. I suddenly remembered my daughter had asked me for a key chain so I scored one there. It's so cute I got myself one too. They're both really special. Everywhere I went I saw crazy expensive souvenirs, just as expensive as everything is in Iceland. Nothing jumped out at me until those key chains did.

At the airport, after I'd gone through a stressful time at duty-free, I remembered I hadn't bought a fridge magnet. I was bummed. No ornament either. After that, I headed down the escalator and boom right there was yet another duty-free. Haha. So I grabbed a water and another special looking magnet of an elf. As I was in line I spotted an ornament but didn't have enough time to get back out of line and I'm sure they were pricey.

I also went to a local pool this morning. I went on a Northern Lights Tour last night and literally felt as though my bones were going to shatter. So I decided the pool today would ease my body tension and relax me before my flight. I was a little disappointed that they use chlorine in the local pools. The Blue and Secret Lagoons do not. It was minimal, but enough to slightly irritate my body.

The Northern Lights Tour irritated me last night too. It was the most unhappy I'd been on my trip. First, it was a tour and I hate tours it turns out. But I booked it last minute because the chances for the lights were good and I hadn't had luck finding them on my own. I hear they were good the night before too from the city even. But I was so exhausted and cold from my day trip that putting on my boots and walking outside seemed like an ordeal I just wasn't up for. I had gone to bed at 11:30 pm instead which meant I'd woken up at 6:30 am. I slept in for a bit and then got up.

A friend I'd met on my Glacier Tour had been texting me and we decided to meet up at the National Museum. More about my friend later.

• • •

My friend from Colorado and I met on an Ice Caving Tour and hit it off. So yesterday I decided I'd drive to the big church I'd been wanting to see first thing in the morning and meet him at the National Museum after. Before meeting him, I'd also visited the Penis Museum. This was high on my list, naturally. Haha

So I drove to the famous Hallgrimskirkja Church and almost got stuck in the snow only to find there was nowhere at all to park. I decided I wasn't meant to see that damn church since I'd tried another day with no luck as well.

Annoyed because now I would have to find the museum and parking, I drove around for what ended up being another 45 minutes. I decided that since the Penis Museum and National Museum were in completely different areas, that I would skip the first and go to it later after horseback riding.

By this time it was nearly 10:00 am so I drove down to park by the National Museum. I finally found parking and walked up to find that it didn't open until 11:00 am on Tuesdays. Not knowing if my friend knew this, I waited around thinking I might run into him, but he wasn't anywhere in sight. So I left, turned the corner and saw the Harpa center! These were all famous places I didn't think I was going to have time to see on this trip since I hadn't spent much time in the city at all.

So once I saw the Harpa Concert Hall, I went with the flow and wandered down there through the snow. I'm so glad I did! It was absolutely beautiful. I got quite a few good pics, probably the best from the trip. I'd braided my hair that day and felt really cute. And based on the fact that I was finally having people notice me, I must've looked cute. Plus my red hair was super visible next to the glaring white snow. The children in Iceland seemed intrigued by this, especially at the pools.

After looking around Harpa it was nearly 11:00 am, so I headed back to find my friend at the museum. I got there and no sign of him. I'll admit I was disappointed. I waited for about 15 minutes and left. I decided that this wouldn't get me down though and that something else must've been in store for me.

I headed in the direction of food before going on my horseback riding adventure. I started up the hill on the main street which again I didn't think I'd even get to check out and boom, there's the church at the top of the hill. I just had to go! So made my journey upwards, going quickly but also checking out the store and restaurants on the way. But it was food or church...and the church won.

I passed a small convenience store and decided I would stop in on the way back to get food to eat in the car on the way to my scheduled Icelandic Horse Ride. I got to the top and took my classic Instagram Reyjakic photos. I didn't go up to the top for "the photo" as the line was long and I was still integrating back into being around crowds after a week on my own. I went back down and got my groceries and ended up going back a different way, yet it felt familiar.

I realized I was finally starting to understand this city. It was time to leave at this point, but I went back to the museum one more time to see if my friend was there. He wasn't. So off to the stables I went!

Later back in wifi land I got a text from him saying he'd been there walking around the museum the whole time and was sorry he missed me. Had I fucked up? I was very sorry I didn't see him again. But even though things didn't work out how I'd planned, things worked out perfectly. Interesting that was my theme of Iceland.

(Side note: Three months later my friend and I met up in Fort Collins, Colorado, shared a quick dinner and reminisced about Iceland)

• • •

The other day I started to write about the day I drove the famous Golden Circle. I want to finish that story.

The Geysir left me unimpressed. I was actually more excited about the moss covered ground around the Geysir and the steam coming up from the mini geysirs all around. In hindsight, I wish I'd spent more time walking around the geysir area. There was definitely a lot more there to explore.

I must've been really put off by all the crowds to want to leave so quickly and I really had to use the toilet as well. Ha! Of course they had a big store there with beautiful trinkets of every kind. I guess I thought I'd find more treasures at the flea market and cheaper prices, so I didn't buy anything at the store, but that wasn't the case at all I'd find out after the fact.

Again looking back I wish I'd spent more time looking through the stores and purchasing the things I did see. In the beginning, I was penny-pinching as well because I was terribly afraid of running out of money.

After the geysir we (not sure why I put "we" there) went to Pingvellir National Park. I got a little confused about where I was as far as what I was looking at. It wasn't until later reading about it that I realized I'd been looking at the split of the two tectonic plates.

I did get some photos, but I didn't go down closer to them. Again the tourists. I do remember the weather really getting to me that day as well. I wasn't as acclimated as I was in the last days. I used the toilet there which I paid a little money to use, even with a card!

Everything in Iceland is paid by debit card. I only got money out of the machine once when I needed to pay cash for a pub crawl. More on the pub crawl later. At the car park I couldn't figure out the machine and a nice guy offered me his ticket. I was so impressed with that.

My therapist said lots of things like that would be happening to me on my trip and she was right.

Then I headed on to see the waterfalls. I'll have to look up the name of them, as I can't remember which ones they were. They were quite impressive though and fun to see.

It was so insanely windy out while I was there and it was really starting to bother me. The wind was frigid and made it hard to enjoy anything outside for too long. There were two ways to look at the waterfalls...going up or going down. I chose to go down. I attempted to use my selfie stick and I wasn't feeling it. Let's be honest, when am I ever feeling a selfie stick? I wish I'd worn my heavier coat too.

After I was done at the waterfalls I was surprised how early it was. They'd said the Golden Circle would take 6-8 hours and I think it only took me about 3-4 hours, not including the drive home. Now I was so cold and loved the Blue Lagoon so much that I was anxious to get to another hot spring asap.

But first I needed to eat. That was probably contributing to my grumpiness. It was kinda cool not having wifi at that moment. I had to actually get out a paper map, my Lonely Planet book and my handy dandy binder I'd organized all my paperwork in back at home.

I looked at what was around and saw that the tomato greenhouse restaurant I'd read about wasn't too far and got really excited. And from there the Secret Lagoon would be really close. Perfect! Both those things I'd hoped to do, but weren't necessarily planned.

The Fridheimer tomato restaurant and greenhouse were heavenly. I walked in and was transported to another time and space. All the tension from the day eased and I felt so relaxed. It was such a lovely place. I got my table for one while lots of people stared, but not in a mean way. Just interesting to see me dining alone.

They had a small menu and I chose the most popular item...unlimited tomato soup and bread. I wish I'd tried the bread, but I couldn't believe how much that soup alone filled me up! And then, of course, I had to splurge on what they deemed the "world's best bloody mary." They were not kidding! It was so sweet and delicious, unlike any other bloody mary and from the tomatoes grown right there in the greenhouse.

I took lots of photos and used the bathroom a couple of times as the laxatives I'd taken to keep me regular on my trip, had kicked in at that point. Haha. There was a tour that had been finishing up when I got there and it was fun to people watch. Everyone there seemed particularly happy, even the wait staff. They were all really nice. Probably the nicest people I met in all of Iceland!

I liked how the waiter even gave a long speech about the restaurant and the greenhouse before the meal. So quaint. And each table had a fresh basil plant on it that you could use scissors to clip off and put in your soup. So charming! Just thinking back to that place makes me happy.

I left there fat and happy as they say. Good food will do that to you. From there, I programmed my GPS to the Secret Lagoon.

I arrived at the Secret Lagoon between 5:30-6:30 pm I'd say. I remember getting to the restaurant at 3:30 pm, happy I'd made it as it closed at 4:00 pm. Okay, so maybe the Lagoon was 5:30ish. In any case, the changing rooms were similar to the Blue Lagoon in some ways but obviously more locals go to this one.

I got a locker with a key on a wristband. I'd taken my awesome travel towel and changed into my swimsuit. Now this place you really do get butt naked in front of everybody. This sort of thing doesn't bother me at all. I think I'm more European in that way. Not in any sexual way at all, but it feels freeing and I felt so unashamed of my body. More Americans need to experience this.

So I took my required shower beforehand and washed off. Then I went out into the frigid winter wonderland. I hung my towel in the designated towel area, which didn't really make sense to me. Just like the Blue Lagoon, the towels are just frozen or wet from snow by the time you're done so what's the point? Haha

When I submerged myself in the water, the temperature was delightfully warmer than the Blue Lagoon. Some parts even almost burned me! I was warned upon entering not to go in the "hot pots" outlying the lagoon as they are *so* hot. The Lagoon itself had that same ambiance with the magical steam coming up off the water. I floated around checking out the different areas.

The whole place was covered in cute green moss. I felt like I was in Lord of the Rings. The bottom wasn't smooth, but full of pebbles and rocks, that felt good as they massaged my feet.

As I wandered, more people kept leaving the later in the evening it got. This was nice. There was a large group, a family I think, with a little girl, taking pictures. I offered to take one with all of them and they appreciated it. It seemed to make them slightly uncomfortable that I was obviously alone and American as they seemed to be.

A little later, the little girl came and talked to me and gave me a pool noodle she'd been using. She asked me my name and we chatted for a bit. Her dad wasn't quite sure what to make of it, it seemed. After they swam away and we said our goodbyes, I felt this wave of sadness move through. Whenever I see kids on vacation this happens to me.

I wondered if it was because I missed my daughter, but I wasn't sure if that was quite it. I just suddenly felt very alone at that moment. Before I knew it, a rush of tears came flooding through me. I was grateful for the mist and steam rising from the Lagoon at that moment. I simply turned around, laid my head down on the rocks and allowed myself to silently weep for a few minutes.

It felt really good and very cleansing to have this release. I'd already been sitting on the edge of the Lagoon where there were rocks forming little benches in various places. It had started to get so hot that I'd been sitting up out of the water a bit and resting. So laying my head down didn't seem odd.

I remember feeling grateful that I could allow myself this moment. That I have those moments often when I travel, but the energy gets pent up because people aren't comfortable with displays of emotion. I feel we would all be a lot more at peace if we would be genuine and true to ourselves in each moment.

But that's certainly not the American way. I have so much to say about the American culture after this trip. Nothing new, but things that further solidify how I already felt about Americans.

After my brief cry, I felt better and since I'd been there, there was a couple circling around and the guy kept looking at me. It made me a bit curious, but I didn't know what to make of it. I watched them taking pictures, or at least *attempting* to take selfies. So again I offered my services. They were grateful and the girl and I struck up a conversation. She seemed happy to have someone to talk to other than her partner.

Turns out they were your stereotypical happy, friendly Canadians from New Brunswick. They were married, but I wasn't sure how long. They referenced being together at least ten years. I definitely looked and felt older than them though. They were small-town folk who seemed to travel frequently.

They commended me for being a mom and still having a life and traveling. I hadn't thought about it like that until then, but it was true.

I started thinking about how many women lose themselves to motherhood. I know I sure had during my marriage. We live in a society where we're always supposed to put our kids first. We mold our lives around what they want and need. And somehow this feels completely backwards to me. What is it we're doing for ourselves as mothers?

So this assurance from a Canadian couple about my personal choices really helped to validate my feelings and decisions about how I was choosing to live my life.

I knew I needed this trip. I knew it would change me somehow, although I wasn't quite sure how yet. It wouldn't be until Snaefellsnes that I would really feel that shift.

Come to find out the couple hadn't planned their trip very well and hadn't even heard about the weather warnings throughout Iceland for the following day. They had big plans to drive North the next day and I assured them it probably wasn't going to be possible.

I thought about them a lot after that, especially the next day when all the roads in and out of the city closed due to high winds. It was surprising to me how many people I'd met throughout the trip that just showed up in Iceland on a whim, with no fixed agenda or planning skills at all.

I couldn't even imagine that at the time. It wasn't until my next Iceland excursion when I'd met my other friend and bonded over the joy of trip planning, that I'd see I wasn't alone.

After several hours in the Secret Lagoon together, we said our goodbyes. I could sense that the girl and I really didn't want to part ways, but the guy seemed to be getting anxious. I took this cue since I was desperately thirsty anyway, and excused myself.

I then took my publicly naked shower, got dressed, dried my hair and made the trek home. It started snowing pretty heavily and got a little hairy at times, but my car did great on the road back to Rekjavik.

Day 1 - Travel
Day 2 - Arrive, Duty-Free, Pick up Rental Car, Drive to Blue Lagoon, Spent 4 hours there. Drove to Airbnb in Reyjavik and checked in after picking up groceries in Bonus.
Day 3 - Golden Circle, lunch at Fridheimer Tomato Greenhouse, Secret Lagoon, Cooked dinner at home.
Day 4 - Stayed in bed until 2pm, went to Elf School from 4-7pm, dinner at Lobstersoup in Old Harbor, walked downtown to the Drunk Rabbit Irish Pub for a pub crawl.
Day 5 - Ice Caving Tour. Crazy day. I got hot dogs with my new friend at 1 am in Reykjavik after the tour.
Day 6 - Record snowfall, walking tour (left midday through), Fleam market, Buffet Lunch at Restaurant Reykjavik. Reykjanes Peninsula drive, Dinner at Hofrin.
Day 7 - Snaefellsness Peninsula (9-hour road trip)
Day 8 - Harpa Church and downtown Reykjavik, horseback riding, Lucky Records, Penis Museum, Kex Hostel for dinner, saw the famous monument across the street.
Day 9 - Local pool, Whales Exhibition, Leave for Airport.
Day 10 - Continued Travel Home

(Side Note: You'll get much more of the actual shadow dances that occurred during this trip in future Adventures of Awakenings books.)

Soak in and feel the magic of this Spotify Playlist I created for Iceland:

https://open.spotify.com/user/1265771279/playlist/3VBedP26X
QEuzHIwFCuYId?si=ROhmlGOOSQGBV3GWOI1azA

Appendix

B

Brussels

(Note: The following is my actual, unedited "cell phone writing" from the airplane on my way home from Brussels, May 2018.)

Picture this.

We arrive at the Brussels airport early Friday morning. It's the last day of a 10-day EuroTrip, en route to Geneva, back to Chicago.

We've already checked in on our phones so we immediately go to the self-check-in. I'd paid to check a bag on the return trip so we figure this should be quick and painless.

Wrong.

In Bruges (the day before), I'd bought a bottle of super unique alcohol that I insisted on taking home with me. This is super odd, to begin with since I don't actually drink, but for whatever reason, I just had to have it. I'm sure it had nothing to do with the actual gold flecks and sparkles it had in it

So checked bag it is.

After the self-check-in, we are sent to a bag drop line, where we wait for what seems like forever. Probably more like 25 minutes.

We get to the front of the cue, scan our boarding passes and it says we have to see an agent.

Not good.

There's no time for this nonsense.

We look around and all we see are the glares of everyone in line behind us. Finally, we catch the eye of the agent, and she sends us to yet another line to speak with another agent. We wait in this line for 30 more minutes!

My blood pressure is rising.

We get up to the front and the woman just looks at us and says "you're late."

I'm dumbfounded. We've just been in lines for nearly an hour!

She tells us we can't check the bag I'd paid for because the plane is leaving soon.

We explain we've been waiting in lines and that we'd like a refund for the bag then. She points and says if I want a refund, I can go wait in another line and miss my flight.

Wow.

I decide not to get the refund and head for security. We stop at the trash bins to throw away the specialty liquids and go towards the lines. We take one look and our bodies shrink a little bit.

There's just no way we will make it.

We ask an attendant if there's any way to get through the line faster as our flight leaves in 20 minutes.

Not just boarding, but leaving in 20 minutes!

She says no, but redirects us to another line at the end that should be shorter.

We get to the end and that line is even longer!

I'm completely starting to lose it at this point.

Now we're in line, attempting to jam my checked bag stuff into the carry-ons.

The whole scene is a hot mess.

Our impatience is building by the minute.

You see, we are actually trying to get to Geneva, Switzerland. Once in Geneva, we're connecting to our flight back to the U.S. There is no way we can miss this flight to Geneva.

We decide to ask another attendant if we can get through as we now only have 10 minutes left. He's much nicer and says to ask the people in front of us.

Luckily, the lady directly in front of us speaks English and says to go ahead. The attendant opens up the line so we get a little further, but not all the way to the front.

There are still 15 more people in front of us!

We finally make it to the security belt and I'm ungrounded, scattered, and can barely function. Not my finest travel moment.

I'm making a bad attempt to take out all the toiletries and electronics and place them on the belt.

I forget my phone in my pocket and set off the alarm as I go through.

Face palm.

Then all three of my bags go through and are pulled aside for inspection.

Of course they are.

My hands are sweating. I'm on the verge of tears.

Turns out the cheese I'd had in my suitcase was a cause for alarm. The agents all make some jokes in French and are taking their sweet time, rifling through my clothes.

It's now 9:17am. Our flight leaves at 9:20am!

After another eternity, we're cleared and start running. I have a massive backpack and a super heavy under-the-seat bag in tow. And I'm running as if my life depends on it.

Naturally, our gate is at the very end of the terminal, which means navigating through the crowds in all the stores, restaurants and other gates.

I can barely breathe.

We get to the gate, begging and pleading our case.

It's too late.

Nope. I won't accept this.

They start making phone calls and we insist we have to make our connection in Geneva.

Then, a miracle happens. Hallelujah!

They stop the plane and wait for us!

It takes everything in me not to break down crying.

Next, we finally board the plane, and for the first time actually look at our tickets. We don't have seat assignments, even though we've paid extra for specific seats.

Can anything else possibly go wrong?

The flight attendant tells us to go to the back and ask the other attendant what to do.

Everyone is staring and frustrated as we are holding up the plane in a big way.

We are hot, sweaty and barely breathing.

The attendant at the back of the plane says she cannot help us and sends us back upfront.

Are you freaking kidding me?!

We head back up front and see two seats, one in front of the other. The flight attendant tells us we can't sit there because people in those seats are provided a meal! I'm in complete shock.

We've made it this far and now we're getting hung up on details?!

We promise not to eat and everyone's up in arms about the situation.

Luckily, the people in the rows we are trying to sit in, come to the rescue!

A couple of businessmen speak English and welcome us into the two last empty seats on the entire plane. We scramble in and sit down.

My eyes well with tears. I'm grateful and exhausted.

I close my eyes and the next time I open them, we are in Geneva.

Moral of the story: Always give yourself enough time at the airport, especially when you are in a foreign country!

Appendix

C

30 Superpowers You'll Acquire
as a Solo Female Traveler
(2018)

Solo female travel is on the rise, and yet it still remains a bit of a mystery.

Do you notice a craving you're feeling deep in your bones for a different kind of travel experience? I've been there. And while solo travel isn't the only way for me, it's a passion of mine to encourage women to get out of their heads and follow the call.

My solo experiences have been deeply profound and life-changing times, and I've gained a whole lot of badass superpowers along the way!

Solo travel can seem daunting, but I promise you, it's much more rewarding than it is scary.

If you've been having doubts about planning some time away on your own, then I hope this list of all the amazing things you have to gain, will inspire you to take that leap of faith.

Whether you go on one solo trip or want to plan many in the months and years ahead, I'm here to support you!

So, here's my list of *The 30 Superpowers You'll Acquire as a Solo Female Traveler*:

Courage – You'll become a courageous travel warrior, who steps out of her comfort zone, and isn't afraid of the unknown.
Strength – Even when you don't feel strong, you'll find you bounce back from challenges more quickly than ever before.
Freedom – There's no holding back from being completely, authentically YOU!
Powerful – If you can save up for a trip, do the research, plan it and put it into action, you'll feel like you can do anything in the world. And guess what? You can!
Increased Intuition – Your intuition increases more and more over time. You start to really listen to that feeling in your body

that tells you when something is right and when it's not. And you let that feeling be your guide.

Deep Self-discovery – You'll gain more knowledge about yourself than you ever knew possible. You'll discover your likes and dislikes more than ever before because it's all about you!

Empathy – Being immersed in other cultures leaves you with a better appreciation for all the cultural differences in the world. You gain a greater ability to understand the feelings of others. Even though our backgrounds and experiences might be different, we can relate on a deeper emotional level.

Bravery – You're ready to face the challenges ahead of you with strength and grace.

Problem Solving – You become an expert problem solver. Challenges will arise, and you have to gain the confidence in yourself to figure it all out on your own. And you will!

Ability to be present – You'll find yourself in many situations where you see or experience something so incredible that, you naturally want to share it with someone else immediately. But over time, you develop the ability to sit with yourself and dive deeper into the experience of being completely present and in the moment. And you'll see that some of the most amazing moments are better experienced alone.

Patience – Your capacity to accept delays and disruptions increases. When we hit a roadblock, we always have a choice to go with the flow or let it get us flustered. You'll find yourself a more patient person overall.

Connection – When you're alone, there's more opportunity to meet and connect with locals or other travelers. Sometimes, these connections can last a lifetime!

Confidence – You'll gain a certainty within yourself after you've conquered some major mountains. Once you've accomplished your goals on your own, you're less likely to doubt yourself the next time. You go from needing external validation to having internal validation.

Increased awareness – Developing a heightened state of awareness happens naturally without others distracting you. You start to notice all the little things, which are usually the most magical.

Discernment – You're able to make quality decisions without judgment.

Positivity – The world is an amazing place! Instead of focusing on the negative side of life, you feel yourself creating a more positive outlook because life is so darn incredible!

Inspiration – Just thinking about travel inspires me. When you're relaxed and in the flow of your travels, you'll be inspired by people, places and experiences.

Creativity – Inspiration leads to creativity. When we're inspired by our surroundings, we're more likely to create works of art, write and express ourselves creatively.

Wisdom – There is an innate wisdom in all of us women. We just have to access it. By traveling alone, honing-in on your intuition, and letting your body guide you, you are allowing this wisdom to flow through you. By experiencing other places, cultures, languages and people, you become the Wise Woman.

Wildness – You don't restrain yourself from being exactly who you are. You let go of control and unleash the authentic, wild woman inside of you.

Trust – You learn to trust yourself more, allowing more of your wisdom to bubble up inside of you. You trust that you're okay. And you trust that you can do it.

Respect for your body – Your body is your guide. When it wants to rest…rest. When the body wants to move…move it in whatever way feels good for you. Spending time alone allows you to really get in touch with your physical needs. Allow that relationship to flourish.

Ritual – Pay attention to the rituals you have in your life. When you're alone, there's more space to take time for daily devotion in whatever way that means for you. Morning yoga, prayer, meditation, sipping warm tea. Notice how your body and soul want to be nourished.

Pleasure – When you're alone, your capacity for pleasure actually increases. Through a heightened state of awareness, you expand your capacity to enjoy being in a feminine body.

Playfulness – When you're relaxed, you're much happier and more playful. And when it comes down to it, the journey of travel can be played as a game. Allow yourself to access that inner child and have uninhibited fun!

Communication skills – You'll find your voice and learn how to use it, a lot.

Openness – Stay open to whatever comes your way. Plans may change, which direct you somewhere else where you find you have an even better time than you'd planned. Being open allows for ease of experience.

Uniqueness – When you're traveling alone in the big world, you start to see just how unique you are, and how unique everyone is! How we all have a part to play and have special gifts only we can offer the world.

Relaxation – By slowing down, we learn to relax into receiving, rather than striving to achieve. We learn that we don't have to buy into the go-go-go culture that encourages us that doing more, faster, is always the goal. We learn to rest, listen to our bodies, quiet our minds and enter a place of deep relaxation we may never have tapped into before.

Celebration – When was the last time you celebrated your achievements in life? Let the experience of solo travel be one of celebration for you. This is your time to shine! Do what makes you happy, always.

ACKNOWLEDGEMENTS

A massive thank you to D. D. Scott for guiding me through the journey of writing, self-publishing and birthing this creation out into the world. Thank you to the sacred sisterhood of women who are currently in my life and to those who are no longer in my life but remain in my heart. And more than anything, my heart is filled to the brim with gratitude for all The Lost Boys.

NOTE FROM THE AUTHOR

I hope you've enjoyed journeying along with me in the Adventures of Awakening: Alchemizing Pain Into Personal Empowerment, Book 1 of my new series of 7 books.

Now that you've read my overall story, each subsequent book in the series will dive deeper into the various parts of my journey of alchemizing pain into personal empowerment. My hope is that it sparks a soul-stirring within you and inspires you to live out your biggest, boldest dreams, while awakening to the truth of who you are on a more soulful level. I can't wait to share more of my personal magic with you!

To be the first to hear about all the magic on its way, my adventures and musings, sign up for my newsletter at: https://www.thekelseydecker.com

If you'd like to embark or continue embarking on your own adventure of awakening with some specific guidance as to how to alchemize your pain into personal empowerment, go to: https://www.thekelseydecker.com/work-with-me-1

If you know of someone who could use the messages I have to share, please share this book with them! And if you enjoyed the book, please leave a review on the site for the store from which you purchased it. That's how other readers find my books! Your reviews make all the difference and mean the absolute world to me!

Also, feel free to email me at: thespiritualtravelagent@gmail.com.

I would love to hear from you!

Thank you so much for choosing my book and happy reading!

Kelsey Decker
October 2019

ABOUT THE AUTHOR

Kelsey Decker is an Author, Speaker, Teacher, Healer and Spiritual Guide. She's a multi-passionate entrepreneur with a background in energy therapy, movement, meditation and digestive health. She's facilitated workshops, women's circles and retreats locally and internationally since 2000. Her passions include travel, transformation and transcendental experiences. She's a single mom to Liliana, the light of her life. She empowers women to embark on the journey their soul has been calling them to take, so they can step fully into an inspired life, become unstoppable and create clarity to live out their biggest, boldest dreams. She considers herself a sacred rebel, conscious creator and magic maker! Kelsey has an infectious, authentic energy that restores joy and vitality to all with whom she connects.

She'd love to welcome you into her communities at:
www.thekelseydecker.com
Facebook The Kelsey Show 2.0
Instagram The Kelsey Decker
Twitter @thekelseydecker
LinkedIn Kelsey Decker
Pinterest The Kelsey Show

BOOKS BY THE AUTHOR

Adventures of Awakening Series:

Alchemizing Pain Into Personal Empowerment (Book 1)
Dancing with The Dark (Book 2) – *Coming Soon!*
Books 3-7 – *Coming Soon!*

Printed in Great Britain
by Amazon